I AM

LEARNING

TO LOVE

I AM

LEARNING

TO LOVE

A Personal Journey to Wholeness in Christ

Martin Hallett

Marshall Pickering

Marshall Morgan and Scott
Marshall Pickering
3 Beggarwood Lane, Basingstoke, Hants RG23 7LP, UK.

Copyright © 1987 By Martin Hallett
First published in 1987 by Marshall Morgan and Scott Publications Ltd
Part of the Marshall Pickering Holdings Group
A subsidiary of the Zondervan Corporation.

British Library CIP Data

Hallett, Martin
  I am learning to love: a personal
  journey to wholeness in Christ.
  1. Christian life
  I. Title

  248.4   BV4501.2
  ISBN 0   551   01316   8

Text Set in Plantin by Brian Robinson, Buckingham.
Printed in Great Britain by Anchor Brendon Ltd, Tiptree, Essex.

Contents

Foreword

At different points in history, God sends his own particular messengers or prophets with a specific word from himself for people living at that moment in time.

The last twenty years has seen an upsurge in openness about homosexuality, a desire for there to be freedom for its physical expression, that sexual equality (ie equality between homosexuals and heterosexuals) should be the norm, and that children in schools should be taught that a homosexual lifestyle is as viable an option as the traditional heterosexual pattern of family life.

The evangelical wing of the Church, in Britain, has by and large shrunk away from the subject. Ignorance, pietistic interpretation of the Scriptures and a gut-level fear of this particular 'unknown' has left homosexual men and women lonely, guilty, rejected and unloved because they have not dared to admit their sexual orientation or they know of someone who has paid for honesty by being shunned.

I believe that God has given Martin Hallett to the Church at a time when she desperately needs him. Not only has Martin been able to share his own pilgrimage into faith, but he has also been able to demonstrate himself that a biblical lifestyle, in which sexual continence is practised, is possible for the Christian.

He understands those 'gay' Christians who feel it is permissible, right and good to have a physical relationship with another Christian, if love and commitment bind them together. Martin, however, cannot reconcile this with biblical teaching and lives out the consequences of such beliefs.

This book is for all, whether 'gay' or not. It will help older teenagers and students grappling with the pull of the 'gay scene'.

Martin Hallett as I have known him over the years is a man of integrity, humility, compassion and loyalty. I believe him to be one of God's messengers or prophets of today. A man whose message must not be taken lightly.

Dr Anne Townsend
Former Editor *Family* magazine
and Former Director, Care Trust

Introduction

'Not another book on homosexuality!'

Well, I hope this one is a bit different. The sharing of my own experiences will inevitably provoke some strong reactions, some very positive and some equally negative. In sharing something of my life with you I have tried to be honest, but have obviously left a lot unsaid. There are many other Christians with a more spectacular story to tell, but nevertheless I hope you will see the work of a wonderfully gracious God.

Many people have been asking me to write such a book as this, in order that Christians may be given more understanding of matters related to homosexuality. It is important to appreciate that because of our uniqueness in God's creation and because of our equally unique experience of life, God deals with us exclusively, in a never-ending process of learning to love: learning to love God, one another and ourselves. However, what I have shared is not simply relevant to those interested in homosexuality. I hope many others will identify with the feelings expressed, whatever their age and sexuality might be.

I am very grateful to so many in True Freedom Trust, who have helped me with this book in terms of prayer, reading and correcting; giving me a place to write it; encouraging me to persevere. A very special thank you to

Anne Townsend for her Foreword and to Edward England for his advice and encouragement.

There are some, however, without whom this would never have happened and I therefore want to dedicate this book to them, for the glory of God. Thank you Tim, John and Michele; Roy and Barbara; Nigel and Linda; Peter and Annette; my father, Cyril Hallett. I love you . . . and I'm learning to love you even more.

Martin Hallett
(September 1986)

1: Schooldays

It was my first taste of boarding school. I had been a 'day boy' since the age of seven, but now, at thirteen I was boarding for the first time. Large Victorian buildings, many of them converted houses, formed a major part of the school's property, but they had been supplemented by one or two more modern buildings. The campus extended over fifteen acres, situated in an older part of Liverpool suburbia. I had lived in this area all my life. It was very familiar territory, except for the boarding houses in the school, which seemed another world.

The dormitory was large, old and drab with thirty iron-framed beds in two rows, facing each other. Each bed, with its own bedside cupboard, was devoid of anything at all homely. Regular inspections by the prefects made sure that the white cotton sheets and coarse blankets were made up meticulously by the envelope method, without unnecessary folds or creases. As we all prepared for bedtime I was filled with a sense of fear, dreading what more horror tonight could bring. It seemed like a nightmare from which I could never awake.

Eventually, having bathed and changed into pyjamas, it was time to get into bed. It had been my turn to use one of the four Victorian baths. Thankfully, I remembered to test the amount of water by sticking my thumb on top of the plug. The water was to be no higher than my wrist. We were also carefully timed, so that we would not try to relax and luxuriate in the two inches or so of hot water. We were made to shower after all sport activities, which took place nearly every day, so we were not really all that dirty.

The lights went out and for a moment or two there was silence. My fear was beginning to increase and I could feel my heart thumping under the bedclothes.

Then a voice from the dark corner of the dorm said, 'Let's have a "cage". Who shall we do tonight?'

My heart missed a beat. 'Oh please God, let it not be me!'

'What about Hallett?' another voice said menacingly.

'Stand up on your bed, Hallett.'

As I nervously stood on the bed a torchlight shone through the darkness. It was followed by one or two others and then they focused their beams on my eyes. In a strange way the dazzling glare from the torchlights provided a physical distraction which somehow relieved just a little of the tension.

'What shall we make him do?'

'I know! . . . Drop your trousers!'

I obeyed immediately, trying not to appear as terrified as I knew I was.

'Now, what will they ask me to do?' I wondered.

'You really are the lowest of the low, aren't you?' the menacing voice continued.

'Say yes, you horrible creature!' someone else chipped in.

I did not reply. I hoped I would play this right and not encourage them to continue. Perhaps if they didn't think I was frightened, they would stop.

'You have been seen talking to the day boys again. You know that's not permitted.'

I remained silent.

12

There seemed to be a little uneasiness. Someone was coming: 'Get back in your bed!' shouted one of the boys.

The torches went out and I obeyed. Seconds later the prefect came in and got into bed. At last I felt a bit more secure. He was the head prefect of the school and seemed more gentle, fair and sensitive than the others. I had to clean his shoes for him once, as a minor punishment and was struck by his lack of arrogance, compared to most of the others. I knew he was one of the few people in the boarding house whom I could look up to and admire. He had all the necessary qualities; he was mature, a good sportsman, tall and quite good looking.

As I lay in bed, I began to wonder how on earth I could ever escape from this seemingly endless nightmare. Up to this point, my life as a 'day boy' had been very enjoyable. I had a few close friends who lived within cycling distance of our house. We lived only a couple of miles from the school itself, which made commuting by bike very easy. In fact, latterly, I was travelling home for lunch, which made a nice break in the day. We often had three mile runs, after lessons at 4.30, but on three afternoons a week we had to play rugger or cricket, which would mean arriving home earlier. Saturdays were taken up with classes in the morning and sport in the afternoon. Membership of one of the cadet brigades was compulsory and most of us were in the Combined Cadet Force, which was run as close to military standards as possible. As a day boy, I quite enjoyed the 'CCF' as it was called – we were able to have quite a bit of fun and sometimes 'send up' our superior officers. It was a combination of the old television series, 'The Army Game' and the more modern equivalent, 'Dad's Army'. The punishments both in the 'CCF' and at school were generally quite severe, but we were able to take them in our stride. I was not a particularly naughty boy, but I enjoyed playing pranks with my mates. There was always a very strong sense of 'fair play' and 'being a good sport'. Telling tales was out of the question and one was always loyal to one's friends.

The reason for a sudden change in my situation was because mother and father had bought a share in a farm, with my uncle, aunt and cousin. It was about thirty-five miles from Liverpool, in Cheshire. The farmhouse was a magnificent Elizabethan mansion, with enough rooms for both families to be self-contained and still have space to spare. It was an exciting contrast to the three bedroomed detached suburban house with which I was familiar.

What made the transition to life as a boarder more difficult was the fact that my parents did not actually move to Cheshire until I had been boarding for a few weeks. This meant I would go home whenever possible in my free time, even though it was out of bounds. We were only allowed to travel within a radius of one mile around the school buildings, and I felt really disorientated visiting my familiar home territory and then having to return to school after only an hour or so. Also, when I was a day boy, it never registered with me that the boarders had made up their own rule of refusing to associate with day boys, a rule I was eventually to transgress.

My brother was an old boy of the school, but because he was thirteen years older than me, he had left long before I had started. He was an actor and occasionally appeared on television and radio. This boosted my ego no end and it obviously impressed the other boys and masters as well. When I became a boarder, his success didn't help me at all, however, perhaps because he had been only a day boy.

I often felt drawn to other boys and the younger masters at school, especially anyone good at sport. One of my best friends Tony, was an active sportsman and often encouraged me to play more effectively. I never really enjoyed sport or was successful at it; I mostly joined in to be accepted. Many times I would see Tony and his friends with their arms around each other. I longed for him to relate to me like that – but he did not.

Even the teachers I admired seemed to be playfully affectionate with the other boys, but not with me. Someone announced that he had read that people who liked men more than women were homosexuals. I found myself blushing because it seemed to describe the way I felt. In fact I could remember having a 'crush' on Richard Burton and Laurence Harvey, whom I met through my brother, when I was only seven. Now, at thirteen I found a book at home on sexuality and read that boys go through a homosexual stage. It crossed my mind that I might grow out of these feelings, although I was not totally convinced that this would happen. Sexual activity with other boys was out of the question for me. I am not sure that I even wanted it very much, it seemed 'dirty'.

Academically, I was lazy and usually accused of not realising my full potential. Unlike my brother, who excelled academically, I was never very far from the bottom of the 'C' stream class. I was often compared to him unfavourably, although I now realise how much I admired him. His strong charismatic personality was something I wanted, but did not have. I think he, in turn, may have felt threatened by my arrival, after thirteen years as a fairly demanding only child. I was very much a dreamer with my head often in the clouds, imagining I had the charisma and eloquence of my extrovert brother.

So I lay in my hard dormitory bed, wondering how my relatively happy childhood could have turned to dark despair. My parents knew how I felt as did the house-master. They were all very sympathetic and felt something should be done to change the situation. The widowed mother of a friend of mine offered to let me stay with them during term time so that I could become a day boy again. This seemed to be the answer to my prayers, but the headmaster refused to allow it. Despite encouragement from my father and mother to 'Try and stick it out, there's a good lad,' I was desperately unhappy. The only strength I seemed to have in this situation was mastering the art of avoiding tears and other physical expressions of my emotions. After years of practice I was very good at not crying. What a terrible mistake many in this generation made in overemphasising a 'stiff upper lip' attitude to every emotional trauma: we suffer for it later.

I may have been quiet, shy and timid but I felt determined that somehow I must do something to bring this nightmare to an end. I decided to run away. Having made the decision to go, it was a few days before I plucked up enough courage to do anything about it. Mother and father had moved to Cheshire by this time and I had nowhere I felt I could escape to. Then one Saturday afternoon was declared free of games. I found myself walking to the station, empty-handed and with hardly any money in my pocket. I very nervously enquired about a train to Chester and was told that if I left my name and address with the station authorities they would send the bill for the train fare to my parents. I felt a sense of tense excitement and relief, as well as some anxiety, as I made the hour long train journey to Chester. It was about twelve miles from there to my new home, on a very busy main road. I walked a few miles to the first village and stopped there, gazing into the river from a pretty road bridge. The full implications of what I was doing started to dawn on me. I wanted to cry, but could not. The best I could manage was a moan and gasp of breath! I continued to walk, then a motorist stopped and offered me a lift, taking me to the end of the long sweeping drive to the house. By this time it was dark and in the shadow of the many shrubberies surrounding the very large front lawn, I was able to sneak unnoticed around the side of the house and then through an open back door. I crept up to the top floor and hid in the attic. There I stayed for what seemed an eternity. I felt secure, it no longer seemed like quite such a bad dream. Eventually I decided to creep into my bedroom, again hopefully unnoticed. Once in bed, I tried to sleep. Mother and father came into the bedroom and said very little, apart from, 'Well, you're a fine one! We'll have to sort this out in the morning. It's too late now . . . We've been very worried!' This must have been an understatement – the school had phoned earlier to ask if they knew my whereabouts!

My parents were sympathetic but took me back to school on the Monday and straight to the headmaster, who said he was prepared to take me back and would not punish me severely, provided I promised not to run away again. As that was a promise I said could not be kept and as he still refused to let me become a day boy it was agreed that I should leave the school. I felt a tremendous sense of relief.

We went to see the Cheshire education authorities and found that I would only be eligible for the local secondary modern school. I was quickly enrolled there, on the understanding that I would leave at fifteen to take my 'O' levels at the Chester College of Further Education.

Life at this country school was a refreshing new experience for me and there were girls there too. I had not been used to relating to women since my early childhood, when I had a few girl friends. However, until the age of seven or eight I can clearly remember wishing I could be a woman, (especially when I had crushes on male film stars!) Later these feelings seemed to evaporate as did an interest in feminine things. I became just like all the other boys and enjoyed playing with cars, trains and planes.

I soon felt very much at home in this school. For the first time in my school career I was near the top of the class, mainly because of my past education. The emphasis on sport was not as strong, although even I was able to show them how to play rugger. In many ways I seemed to be respected and accepted, partly because of my grand home and school background. It was also at this time that I became aware of a sexual interest or curiosity in some of the other boys, rather than just emotional feelings. In the public school we were used to one another's bodies, as we bathed and showered together. However, these boys were much more modest and shy as far as their bodies were concerned and this made me feel the same way. Perhaps this accounted for the sexual curiosity that developed in me and, possibly, in one or two of them.

After about eighteen months, the time came for me to move to college in Chester for my 'O' levels.

One of the understandings, when we moved to the farm, was that my father would not have to work as hard at the bakery business in Liverpool. Sadly, this arrangement had not worked out and he made the difficult journey every day. This became a strain on him and a worry for my mother, so reluctantly it was decided that we should move back to Liverpool and a house was bought. I then began commuting to college in Chester from Liverpool.

College life was far less disciplined than school and it was not long before I began to take advantage of this. If I missed my train in the morning I would spend the day wandering around Birkenhead or Liverpool, arriving home at the normal time. My sexuality was certainly developing now and I knew I was definitely interested in men. However, I found it difficult to believe that they would be interested in me until I was older, because at sixteen my voice had still not broken. A fascination with the male physique encouraged me to start buying bodybuilding magazines, which were supposedly for athletic interest, but I think were really produced for homosexuals. They were the equivalent of 'girlie magazines'. This was before the days of blatant homosexual pornography but, nevertheless, interest in these magazines soon became something of an addiction. I used to hide them at home, but I know mother discovered them at various times, although nothing was ever said. I guess she must have been very concerned, but possibly thought it was part of my 'growing up process' – this was the early 'swinging sixties'. It was at this time that I discovered a place in Liverpool, near my bus stop, where homosexuals met for sexual relationships. There was no social contact, it was simply a place for importuning. I was fascinated, but too shy to get involved. I found myself frequently drawn back to this place and others I soon discovered, but never plucked up enough courage to 'go off' with anyone.

I had an active imagination and at this time used to pretend I was a famous singer, with lots of money, buying Rolls Royces and large houses for my family and myself. A lot of this had developed because of my brother's theatrical influence – I had been taken backstage, since I was seven and had met several famous people. The major problem was that I was so shy I would hardly ever speak to anyone, unless spoken to, and my fantasy world seemed very unlikely ever to become reality. Perhaps it was the extrovert within seeking to break out! I remember once overhearing my father talking to one of the teachers from the secondary modern school, saying, 'I'm worried about

Martin, he doesn't seem to have anything about him!' I think this would have been the general impression given by my quiet, shy nature. I never used to swear or blaspheme and had a vague idea about God's existence. I used to pray every night, just in case he was there somewhere. I also avoided walking under ladders; kept my fingers crossed and read the horoscopes – to keep all the options open! I wanted good things to come my way. I had been to Crusader classes in Liverpool many years earlier and even went to a big celebration with them at the Albert Hall in London. However, the spiritual content and teaching must have gone straight over my head, because the only thing I can remember is looking at the torn and tattered curtains on the stage of the community hall where we met and wanting to rearrange them, so that they would look more theatrically aesthetic! This is no reflection on the Crusader class. The leaders were warm and caring but somehow the teaching did not penetrate my brain. My parents were always saying, 'We must go to church more often', but they never did and it remained a resolution that only really bore fruit after I became a Christian twelve years later.

It was not surprising that I failed all my 'O' levels and father felt I should go away to college in Blackpool to get some qualifications for the bakery business. Then at least I would have something to show for all my schooling. I agreed and was soon lodging in a homely boarding house in Blackpool with two other students from the College of Food Technology. They were in the Hotel and Catering Department and I was in the Bakery College.

Before long I began to get very emotionally involved with one of my fellow lodgers, Simon, and we became very close friends. He was a gentle and sensitive person. I longed to share my feelings with him, but was too scared.

I wondered if maybe he felt the same way. Could he have homosexual feelings as well?

One day, I decided to take the plunge and wrote him a note explaining something of my feelings, without using words like 'homosexual'. I still refused to use that kind of identity, although I frequently felt myself blushing if the word was mentioned, or expressions like 'queer' or 'fairy' were used on conversation. The note was left in Simon's bedroom with a copy of a male photo magazine called *The Young Physique*. It was fairly cryptic and simply said, 'I think you ought to know that I am interested in this kind of thing . . .' I was of course hoping that he was as well. Simon did not come running along to me with open arms and say, 'Martin, I feel like this too!' His reaction was not really what I expected. He said that he did not mind me feeling like this, but if I was to continue as his friend, then others must not know about me, in case they suspected that he might be a 'queer'. He warned me about the way one or two others in the college like that were ostracised. He advised me to watch the way I walked and sat down. That is, not with legs tightly crossed, in an effeminate manner, but both feet on the floor, knees wide apart! Simon's fears were accentuated because some more students from his department were about to move in the next day. The following evening I worked really hard on the 'macho' image. I managed to stop crossing my legs all evening and was surprised how easy it seemed to be. Simon came up to me later and said in a very affirming manner, 'Martin you managed really well. Keep it up!'

Simon and the new lodgers, Gavin and Tony, were always talking about their female conquests. Simon was obviously the least experienced and somewhat in awe of the other two, with a childlike admiration. One evening a trip to the cinema was arranged and a girlfriend allocated for me. This was not the first time I had taken out a girl. I had shown a little interest in a girl at the secondary modern school, but nothing had really developed in the way of a relationship. At that time I was to some extent hoping to prove to myself that I was 'normal', but now it was probably just to be accepted by Simon and his friends.

I was determined to prove myself and had nearly every move carefully planned, although it really seemed like an ordeal. Before very long I took the plunge and put my arm around Susan's shoulder. She moved her head towards mine and I was predominantly aware of her false eyelashes tickling my cheekbone. I could not concentrate on any of the film (a two and a half hour epic) because of my self-consciousness and concern about my next move! I did not enjoy the experience at all, but it served a very important purpose for me. I was now much more accepted and trusted by the others. Simon came to me afterwards with a look of admiration on his face and said 'You were all right there! – I saw you – you didn't waste any time, did you? You were the first to make a move! I was really proud of you.' He also made a point of exclaiming to the others, 'Did you see Martin – eh! There's nothing wrong with him is there?'

I soon discovered to my horror that Susan was known as easily available for sex and what was even worse, she fancied me! I managed to convince the others that I did not really like her type anyway and avoided any other 'heavy' relationships with women, whilst still keeping Gavin and Tony 'off the scent'. Many times I would be alone with Simon in the car and long for his affection. We frequently drove to my home in Liverpool or his in Northumberland, for a few days together. The nearest my dream ever came to reality was when on a long overnight coach journey from Blackpool to London, he fell asleep and his head fell onto my shoulder. It felt ecstatic, even though I was a little self-conscious.

After two very happy years in Blackpool, I moved back to Liverpool to work in the family bakery business. Having got my National Bakery Diploma, I still knew no-one else with homosexual feelings.

2: A New Lifestyle

Back in Liverpool, only a couple of my friends had not moved on to university or college. A few were still in Chester, but it was too far just to drop in and see them. By this time, I had my own car, a Volkswagen, and, at a loose end, began to drift towards the places of sexual interest I had discovered on my way home from school. While at Blackpool, my voice had broken. I was eighteen at the time and now felt more confident that I was old enough to be sexually attractive to another man. I started meeting people in these places of sexual importuning, but still had no sexual or even social contact with them. We would just agree that there was nowhere to go for sex and I would disappear. I was still very nervous.

Then, one weekend, my parents had gone away and I had the house to myself. I went out for the evening and met a guy called Hans, who claimed to be German, and took him home. He was about twenty-eight and a rather mysterious character, and I found him very attractive indeed. After our encounter I longed to meet up with him again. I realised I did not have his address or phone number so several times went out to search for him. By this stage I had experienced a few brief sexual encounters, but I had never met anyone I wanted to see again.

Eventually I tracked Hans down again, and he revealed

to me that he was not in fact German but an English schoolteacher and his name was Geoff. He was involved with another man called John. Geoff eventually asked me if I had ever been inside 'one of the "gay pubs" in Liverpool'. I said 'no', but felt curious to see what they were like. I was very nervous and hesitant to go into one of these places on my own. However, one night I plucked up the courage and was surprised to see how well appointed the pub seemed to be. It was called The Magic Clock and when I looked around I spotted Geoff and his friend John, sitting in a corner. The pub was full of people and had a man in his fifties with a white coat and a pronounced limp standing by the door, as if on guard. In fact, I soon learned that his job was to look out for any potential trouble-makers and keep them out.

I got to know Geoff quite well and used to drive him and John around. We had an almost daily routine. Geoff would meet John in town and go to The Magic Clock. Then I would arrive at about 9.30 or 10.00 pm, have a drink with them and sometimes one or two others. We would leave in my car, with Geoff and John holding hands in the back seat. After we had dropped John off, I would drive Geoff home and we would usually have some sort of sex play in the car together. We also used to talk for hours. Sometimes I would not arrive home until 3.00 am. Considering I was up for work at 5.00 am, it meant I soon became very run down physically. I used to convince my father that I was not tired and encouraged my parents to believe that I had not been all that late coming home. I kept myself going with caffeine tablets, strong coffee and a long rest in the afternoon, after work. I went to bed between 3.00 pm and 4 o'clock in the afternoon, got up at about 7.00 or 7.30 in the evening, dressed and went down to the pub at 9.00. Occasionally, when not with Geoff and

John, I would get involved in other sexual relationships. My strong sexual feelings for Geoff, however, had grown into a very deep emotional attachment. My parents met Geoff and John, plus one or two other friends I had made from the pub. At this stage, I was trying to convince them that it was a coffee bar I was visiting.

Needless to say, Geoff was not really attracted to me sexually, even though I knew I could arouse him. In turn I started to meet a few more people who showed a lot of interest in me sexually, but I was not really attracted to them; in fact I never met anyone else as attractive to me as Geoff. John knew about my feelings and relationship with Geoff, but it did not seem to bother him. He showed very little real emotional interest in Geoff. How I longed to be loved by Geoff, as much as he loved John.

I now spent very little time with any of my friends who were not homosexual. Most of them were no longer in the area. The only sense of real duplicity I felt was in my secrecy at home and also at work. I wanted to be accepted by the workers in the bakehouse and started swearing, blaspheming and telling obscene jokes. They thought, as far as I know, that I was a womaniser. They called me 'the Whoremaster'. There were times when jokes were made about 'queers' and my heart would miss a beat. Sometimes they told me that I should go down to the Magic Clock 'for a laugh at the queers'. I occasionally worried in case I bumped into any of the bakehouse staff in the pub, but tried to keep a convincing story in my mind, just in case I was spotted. I knew that the doorman was very careful about letting 'sightseers' into the pub.

I still said my prayers, believe it or not, but in very much the same attitude of mind as before. If, sometimes, I had a twinge of conscience, I would overcome it by saying, 'Oh I'm sure God doesn't mind'. I used to pray that I would meet attractive people and then use a few other prayers hopefully to make it sound religiously good. Having said that, I never really thought about God at all seriously. As before, it was as if he was a sort of 'good luck charm' for me to try, along with anything else in the same realm.

Occasionally, I travelled to Manchester to a pub there and on one occasion met someone called Tony. He was quite good looking, but without Geoff's athletic physique and I was not aware of a strong sexual attraction for him. Despite this Tony made it clear that he was interested in me and I started to develop a relationship with him. Tony was a romantic and would often write poems to me and send love letters. It was nice to feel wanted and needed. We were always together at parties and in the pub. We went on a short holiday, staying in an hotel in Wales. It was all a new experience for me. Tony's mother encouraged the relationship and loved to make sure we were tucked up safely in bed together. This was because he had been fairly promiscuous and often brought people home for a 'one night stand'. Now, it seemed he wanted to be faithful to me. I enjoyed the romance and the sense of belonging to someone, but I still had much stronger feelings for Geoff, whom I was still seeing.

Tony got a job at the Magic Clock as a barman and I knew that my parents would have to know something, by this time. I was often staying away from home at weekends while I was with Tony. Then came my twenty-first birthday party, and I would be expected to invite many of my friends to this. I told my parents that Tony was working at a pub in town, called the Magic Clock and explained that it used to have a reputation, but was now owned by a respected catering firm, that my parents knew well. (This was in fact true, because this firm had thought at one time of opening it as a restaurant.) I think I managed, to some extent, to pull the wool over their eyes. My parents had experienced a lot of worry because of my brother's psychological and personality problems and it concerned me that they might think my life was going in the same direction.

I took my relationship with Tony very much for granted and I guess really used him to satisfy my own ego and need to feel wanted. It was good to go to parties with a partner and not appear alone. There was a sense in which I was proud to 'belong' to someone and show others that I was worth something to someone else. It is difficult to describe the sense of comfort and security this brings, but I am sure it is comparable to the heterosexual boy and girlfriend relationship. At that point it was these feelings of security, which seemed more apparent than any sense of 'being in love' with Tony.

One evening a friend said to me, 'Martin, you know unless you change your attitude to Tony and respond to him more you will lose him. You can't keep holding up a candle to Geoff forever'. This really struck home and over the next day I chewed over the implications of all that had been said to me. I realised that now I was very frightened of losing Tony. He meant more to me than I thought and I started to panic, making moves to ensure the stability of our relationship. The first step was to buy him a very attractive ring from Liverpool's best jeweller. This meant a lot to him but did not prevent the inevitable change in our relationship. Because Tony now felt secure with me, he began flirting with other people, which was not very difficult, working behind the bar of the Magic Clock, where a high percentage of the customers showed some sexual interest in him. At times I would arrive late at the pub and know for sure that he had been involved sexually with someone else. He would usually get slightly drunk before he could face me, but then it almost seemed as if he wanted me to know about his unfaithfulness, and had a strange sadistic desire to hurt. He would deliberately introduce me to his lover, with a very 'knowing' look on his face as if the two of them had a secret they did not want me to share. My stomach would turn over in the pain of fear, insecurity and jealousy. Then Tony would try to make it up to me by playing sentimental songs over the pub's music system, often in tears to prove I was the only one who really mattered to him. On occasions he would temporarily reject me until he sobered up. Whatever happened, it was a very painful experience, with which anyone having an unfaithful lover can identify.

One of the most difficult situations I experienced with Tony was when on holiday in Majorca. I wanted us both to steer clear of any homosexual company, because of the threat of Tony's unfaithfulness. However, inevitably, Tony persuaded me to go into the homosexual bars with him. At first there were no problems and we also mixed socially with some of the married couples on the package holiday, which pleased me, of course. One evening, Tony was a little drunk and met a guy he wanted. This person's friend wanted me and Tony thought this was a great idea. As far as I was concerned it was certainly not on. Tony got angry and tried to bring his partner into our hotel room. Amazingly, I plucked up enough courage to persuade the hotel porter to ask the stranger to leave. For the rest of the holiday, Tony decided to ignore me. It was a very difficult and traumatic experience; in fact every time I went anywhere near those homosexual bars, the hurt made my stomach turn over.

We had noticed another person in the hotel, whom we suspected of being homosexual. Tony occasionally spoke to him, but because of my determination to avoid anyone else like that, I avoided him. He was obviously from our area, because he flew with us from Liverpool airport. A few weeks later, on our return home this person appeared in the Magic Clock and came over to speak to me. He simply said that he had seen the situation between Tony and me on holiday and wanted me to know that he was disgusted at the way I had been treated. He introduced himself as John and said, 'You deserve better than that. Why do you hang around a place like this? If you ever want to get away, come over to my place in Southport'. After a lot of tears, Tony and I parted company. It was the first time I had cried for many years. Despite all the hurt, I did not want us to part.

I took John up on his invitation and met a whole new circle of friends. They were all homosexual, but did not spend their time in the pubs and clubs. Many had really beautiful houses and we often had dinner parties, went to the theatre and holidayed together.

Ironically, a few months after we parted, I met Tony one evening and he asked me to give him a lift home. He wanted us to sleep together – 'for old time's sake' and I agreed. It seemed as if he might have thoughts of re-kindling our relationship. I was astonished at my reaction, a few months earlier it would have been the answer to my prayers. Now I felt quite differently and almost cold in my emotional response to him. I did not want the hurt and insecurity I experienced before. Time had healed a lot of the hurt – but, as I discovered years later, not all.

Within this new circle of friends, there were six of us who were especially close. Some had stable relationships, having been together for many years. They seemed very much to me like married couples. They had set up home together and very rarely went into a 'gay pub' or club. This was to avoid sexual temptation or unfaithfulness.

Many of the couples that had been together for a long time had an arrangement whereby one partner would be allowed to go off occasionally for another sexual encounter. However, social involvement in these sexual situations was rare, because any emotional attachment would present a threat to the stability of these long term relationships.

I was fairly promiscuous sexually, although I know that I was really longing for a more lasting and stable relationship. With this underlying desire at the back of my mind, sex was something of a hobby. My friends and I frequently shared stories of our sexual conquests. Providing no-one was hurt and an existing relationship was not harmed in any way, we had no strong conviction that this way of life was wrong. There was a tremendous sense of loyalty between us. For example, if I became emotionally involved with someone and the relationship did not work out, my friends would contact me to see if I was all right. They would invite me round, or call in, to make sure I was coping. By this time, I was buying my own house and lived alone for most of the time. One of my close circle of friends, Richard, lived only a few miles away, but the others were about three quarters of an hour's drive into Lancashire. Richard was probably over twenty years older than me, but we never really thought much about it. He was very much the 'English country gentleman' and, although our family backgrounds were very different, we enjoyed one another's company. He was very houseproud and always repairing and decorating. He helped me in many practical ways in my own home. We often went to the theatre and concerts together and sometimes to places where we thought we might make 'a sexual pick-up', but there was no sexual involvement between us. I missed Richard when his job took him to Birmingham. However, my other friends did not allow me to get too lonely, even though they were quite a distance away. From time to time we would meet new people, either through a local club, or a mutual friend.

My social life was therefore quite fulfilling. Mother and father were now much more involved with my friends than ever before. They liked them very much and my friends accepted them in turn. I had still not told my parents about my homosexuality, and although I guessed they probably knew it still seemed something of a difficult subject for me to broach.

My lifestyle could be compared to some extent with the heterosexual playboy, enjoying an active social life, but always on the look out for an attractive appearance, so that I would be a 'good catch' for someone. This, however, was not as apparent as in some parts of the homosexual community, where one can see a real 'rat race' to compete against one another in the 'sexual stakes'. The desire to be attractive can become all consuming, a form of self-idolatry. A need to feel that 'I am beautiful and can therefore accept myself', easily leads to narcissism. It has been said that in all homosexual love there is an element of narcissistic feelings: 'Just as a parent loves his children because they spring from himself and resemble himself, so the homosexual loves the person who is either like himself or else seems to be the man he would like to be'.[1] I used to find that the long lasting homosexual relationships were ones in which the two people involved were different in many ways. They complemented one another, rather than competing or trying to be as physically attractive as each

[1] *Sexual Deviation* by Anthony Storr (Pelican) p 88.

other. One of my major problems in forming a lasting homosexual relationship was that I felt I needed a 'masculine' type of partner, whereas the majority of people who were attracted to me were seeing in my physical appearance, just such a 'masculine' image.

Many of those I met had a deep concern for others and a high standard of 'moral' behaviour, even though I was to learn that it was not really in accord with Christian standards. For example, if someone was involved in a sexual relationship that he did not want to become deeply emotional, he would make that clear to his sexual partner and possibly even break off the relationship. This was so that the other person involved would not get hurt. Discretion was also a keynote within my own circle of friends. We would often meet quite well known public figures, especially from the world of entertainment. We never talked about their homosexuality, or even mentioned that we had met, in case it caused them problems.

I was popular with my friends and there was a very deep sense of love, commitment and therefore loyalty between us. We were not in any way flaunting our homosexuality. In fact at times, especially with relatives and friends who did not know about us, we revelled in the 'undercover secrecy'. The knowing glance to each other, when in so-called 'straight' company, and the use of a language, partly from the theatrical world, which was at this time just becoming more generally known. Words such as 'gay', 'camp',[2], 'drag' and many others could be used quite often with a double meaning. This all helped us to take life and ourselves far less seriously than perhaps we might have done. It has often been said that the use of the

[2]'camp' – flamboyant or effeminate.

word 'gay' is a lie when referring to homosexuality, but I would have disagreed because in my situation, at this time I would say that there was much gaiety, as in the original meaning of the word. I had developed a lifestyle that was fulfilling and pleasant for me and for my close friends. Needless to say, it was selfish and self-centred. We did very little to help others, or the world in which we lived although I must stress that is far from being the case with other people in the homosexual community. I know many work very hard for the good of others in self-sacrificing ways.

What reason did I have to believe that my secure little world was not what God wanted for me? None, as far as I could see. I had good friends, a happy social life, a nice home and car plus a secure job. It would have been nice to be the famous singer and performer of my fantasies, but I was living in the real world now and it was pretty good. There was one gap in my life that I really longed to be filled. I wanted a lover to whom I was attracted and with whom I could live and share my life. I had already seen something of that with my friends, but somehow it never really worked out for me. Deep down I realised that I set my standards far too high and was reaching for the impossible, but still that hope lay not too far beneath my consciousness. It was my prayer to a God whom I hoped might be there.

I had a reputation for holding good parties, especially when they were fancy dress. It was great fun making the costumes for those who did not hire Roman centurions or Regency buffs from the theatrical costumiers. It was also an opportunity to make new friends, as guests were often brought along. One such person was Ken. He was from London, tall, slim and obviously quite an extrovert. There was, however, a sense in which I felt Ken was holding back. He was not the sort of 'high powered London queen'[3] I would have expected him to be. They usually try to impress with all that is happening in London's large homosexual subculture and often make us northerners feel that we are about twenty years behind their development and sophistication. Ken apparently knew that this would be the impression he was expected to give and therefore kept a very low profile. He actually preferred our way of life, in the north, feeling it was much more genuine and less pressurised than the 'London scene'. He was thinking seriously of giving up a very lucrative job in London and moving to Merseyside to work as a poorly paid technician in a local hospital. His only reservation was that he would miss the opera at Covent Garden (a major love of his life). Ken eventually moved to Merseyside and I began to know him quite well.

Many of my friends had to give me a heavy push when it came to meeting others socially, with a view to a relationship. I was very shy and found it almost impossible to take the initiative, when in a pub or club. One evening, Ken came up to me with a rather shy, but nice looking man. He was not physically tall and overpowering, which I normally found attractive, but there was something nice about him. Ken said, 'Martin, I want you to meet Tim'. Then, with a twinkle in his eye, because he knew it would appeal to me, he added, 'Tim is a rugby player'. We started talking and it seemed clear that Ken had met Tim the night before and been to bed with him. Tim did not stay very long, but said that he would see me in there again. He seemed very shy and not

[3] A 'queen' is a term used in the homosexual subculture (and elsewhere) to describe a fairly effeminate and arrogant homosexual. Sometimes it simply refers to a more 'passive' or effeminate homosexual.

environment. Later Ken asked if I liked him and said that he would 'see what he could do for me'. He obviously liked him as well, so his offer seemed very unselfish. He did point out that Tim was very new to all this and therefore needed a lot of encouragement. I decided that I would quite like to meet him again.

3: Meeting with Christ

The Bonaparte was the name of the club in which I had been introduced to Tim. There were several large rooms in the business section of Liverpool City Centre, which were leased for private parties. The rooms that formed the Bonaparte were licensed, but rented by the people running it. One evening at about 9.30 I arrived to find Tim there on his own. With some hesitation, in case he did not want to see me, I walked over to him. 'Hello, can I join you?' I said nervously. 'Yes, let me get you a drink,' he replied in a very sophisticated southern accent. I thought he sounded a bit like someone from the Royal Family! Luckily Richard, the friend who moved to Birmingham, also had a very 'upper crust' type of voice and an eccentric flamboyant manner to go with it so some of my inferiority complexes had already been overcome in that relationship. Tim's manner was so gentle, shy and loving that my nervousness was slowly being overcome. It seemed that he had recently moved to Birkenhead, near Liverpool, in his job as a trainee manager. A few weeks before, while living near Preston, he met another homosexual, also from Liverpool. They had a fleeting relationship but it was the first time Tim had experienced anything like it or met another homosexual, socially. He was hurting inside quite a bit, 'I really don't know if this is

the sort of life I want,' he said. 'It's all very strange to me.'
I tried to assure him that before very long it would all
seem quite natural and normal. The first time I went to a
homosexual party I remember feeling that it was all very
strange, but that soon changed, when I became used to the
environment. Tim did not seem totally convinced, as I
shared my experience with him, but I felt determined that
I would prove to him how right I was. He did not wait for
the club to close, before leaving to catch the river ferry to
Birkenhead. A couple of nights later, he was in the
Bonaparte again and I asked him, along with a few others,
to come to my place for coffee. He agreed and seemed a bit
more willing to talk.

When we were apart from the others in our group, it
seemed easier to talk and he told me that he really had
been 'smitten' by this man in Preston and was finding it
difficult to recover from his feelings of hurt. I tried to
convince him that I could identify with his experience,
and I wanted to offer help and comfort. Then Tim said,
'Martin, I know you will think this sounds silly, but I'm
really not at all sure that this way of life is right. You see I
am a Christian.' I was quite touched by what I thought
was his naivety. I said 'Well I'm a Christian too, but I'm
sure it's OK. They do say all sorts of leading clergymen
are gay and pick up people for sex. I honestly wouldn't
worry about that. I'm sure I've heard stories about all sorts
of famous clergymen!' I repeated my point and laughed.
Tim did not seem impressed at all. He obviously was not
convinced. I decided to take him under my wing and seek
to prove how right and good my lifestyle was. I would
introduce him to my closest friends. After all, his
experience of the homosexual lifestyle was very limited
indeed. It also seemed clear to me that I must not make
any strong moves towards him myself, in case it frightened

him off. I really did not know whether he was interested in me or not. He was obviously in a very delicate state emotionally and not ready for another relationship just yet.

But there was something very appealing about this Tim who called himself a Christian. We had a pleasant, but quiet evening, with the others in my house. Tim seemed a bit more relaxed at my home and said he had never met anyone living alone in their own house like that before. Apparently his parents did not know anything about his homosexuality, neither did his sister, Jane, nor brother-in-law Andrew, whom he said were also Christians. He was very close to them and would like them to know about himself, one day. It was actually his ambition to be married and have a family. 'I love children,' he said, 'and, besides, all my school chums are getting married . . . with all the excitement and preparations, it just makes me long for it myself.' That was a feeling I could not pretend to share or appreciate.

I decided to have a party, so that I could help Tim see how much fun there was for him in our type of lifestyle. It was to be one of my fancy dress parties and I invited all the friends I knew who would make it go with a swing, especially two of my friends from Manchester. They both used to perform and mime Judy Garland, Liza Minnelli or Marlene Dietrich records, when sufficiently drunk. They hardly had an ounce of rhythm in their bodies but the act was so funny I used to be quite sore with laughter, probably because I knew them so well and it was such a contrast to their 'respectable image'. Before this party I was able to spend quite a bit of time getting to know Tim. He said little more about his Christian beliefs, but I sensed he was holding back in some way. There seemed to be sincerity and simplicity there that was quite different from other 'religious' people I had met. My brother had been converted to Roman Catholicism about eight years earlier and the conversations that he and his friends had about religion were almost completely incomprehensible to me. It just seemed like another brand of intellectualism. Also my brother, being very prone to melodrama became totally obsessed with the altar he made in his bedroom, filling the house with the fumes of the incense he continually burned. His friends, the priests, told my parents that his long religious rituals were quite unnecessary.

At this time my relationship with my brother was not at all good. I think I probably hated him, because of all the hurt and upset he had brought to my parents through heavy drinking and extravagant living. Hence I found it very difficult to take his religion at all seriously. It was one more facet of his lifestyle that alienated him from me. I never stopped to think that my parents could have been also worried about *my* lifestyle! Certainly it became clear later, that my attitude to my brother worried my mother a lot. She never really showed her deepest feelings and anxieties and I rarely stopped to think that there might be any there, apart from the obvious ones concerning my brother.

The other religious people I had met were very 'straight laced; non-drinking and serious' people. At least that is the way I viewed them then. Later my impression changed considerably.

So my idea of Christian people was that some were rather dull and boring (although I had a sneaking respect for them) while others seemed to be trying desperately to prove to people like me how ordinary and normal they were. They drank, smoked, swore and did not even seem too bothered about sexual promiscuity. Tim was therefore, very different from anyone else I had met before who claimed to have a faith in God.

The plans for the party were slightly changed in that it was decided it would not be fancy dress. There really was not enough time to prepare for this and in any case I thought Tim would probably find it more difficult to cope with.

As the party got under way, Tim seemed fairly relaxed and at home. By this time he had begun to know quite a few of the people there and was making friendly conversation with some and able to joke with others. Normally, at these parties we would drink as much as was available. Certainly I found it always helped my self-confidence to have a drink continually in my hand. Because I felt Tim was probably even more shy and timid in this situation than he was normally I tried to make sure his glass was always being filled, but was surprised by the fact that he frequently refused more drink. I knew in his situation I would have needed it to boost my self-confidence. I desperately wanted Tim to experience the enjoyment I felt at these events, especially when I had managed to persuade my friends from Manchester to perform for us. It took a lot of careful planning and plenty of alcohol to bring them to the point of doing their 'turn'. They really enjoyed themselves and, as usual, I was convulsed in laughter, but Tim did not seem tremendously impressed, only a little amused. The party ended, with most of us feeling it had been a success, and Tim drove a few people home. He had enjoyed himself, whilst remaining completely sober, but I felt there had been little development in our relationship.

A few weeks went by with no change in the situation. I was now beginning to feel much more strongly that I wanted a very special relationship with Tim, but for some reason it seemed much more of an emotional desire, rather than a sexual one. I had not made any sexual advances towards him, nor was I burning up with a lust to do so. It may have been because I doubted that Tim was interested in me sexually, although I did not know for sure that this was the case. Eventually I asked him to the theatre for my birthday, and he accepted. The day before our trip I was feeling particularly low and discouraged as far as this new relationship was concerned. I had not really given any thought to Tim's religious beliefs, and in fact he said very little more about them. At about nine o'clock I decided to go out for a drink to cheer myself up. Instead of making my usual trip to Liverpool, I went to Chester for a change. At that time the gay bar in Chester was part of a smart hotel in the centre of town. I met a couple of acquaintances there and one gay seemed quite keen to 'take me home'. I declined his offer and decided to make my own way home alone. While driving down a country road on that chilly March evening I felt a wave of depression hit me. I thought to myself, 'What on earth am I doing with my life? Where am I going?' Thoughts of Tim came into my mind. I was in love once more. I said, 'Oh God why is this happening all over again?' Thoughts of many experiences of unrequited love came into my mind . . . 'Oh God, not again!'

Immediately a voice within said, 'Don't worry, Martin. I have brought Tim into your life . . . for you.'

I was stunned. 'Was that God speaking? – or me?' I felt a strange sense of peace within and real hope. It seemed I could continue to relate to Tim. I wanted to throw out any doubts that lingered, in case God really had spoken to me. There was a new found joy in my heart but after a while another thought suddenly struck me. 'If that really was

God, I'd better try to be good – try to know more about him – otherwise he could take Tim away!' I put the car away and went to bed with an instinctive feeling that this was a new beginning in my life.

The next morning, my birthday, I went to work in a rather subdued mood. I still was not sure just how to react to what had happened in the car the night before, but I sensed a kind of 'presence' with me and a peace within. I was still a bit suspicious, in case this was just all a part of my imagination, spurred on by wishful thinking. That afternoon, after work I decided to make a step towards God and thought I would read the Bible. It was not difficult to find the Bible my uncle had given me when I was christened. It had remained on the bookshelf, almost untouched, for many years. I can remember looking through it a few times when I was a child and liking the rich colourful pictures on glossy paper. It always seemed to have a very special smell, slightly sweet and certainly different from any other book. I started to read the Gospel According to St Matthew, which seemed a logical place to begin in the New Testament. I started to read, 'The book of the generation of Jesus Christ, the son of David, the son of Abraham. Abraham begat Isaac; and Isaac begat Jacob . . . ' This really was a new experience for me, but there was something very challenging and exciting about it. In a way, the archaic language of the Authorised Version added to the mystique of this new experience. Somehow the words and their sense were not as difficult to understand as I had always imagined. There was certainly something very special about this book.

The following day I had a very pleasant evening with Tim and he bought me a tie for my birthday, which meant a lot to me. I said nothing of the experience the night before, but mentioned that I had started reading the Bible.

Then Tim told me, with some hesitation that he wanted to see someone about his homosexuality. I was still puzzled by his reaction to sexuality. I did not want to say too much about my own thoughts, as far as God was concerned, until I could understand them myself. I was a bit wary of him thinking that I wanted to move too quickly in the relationship. Again and again, my friends had warned me to 'play it cool'.

The next step I decided to take, in trying to please God, was to go to church. This was a mighty and difficult task for me to undertake. I made up my mind to go in the evening, so that I would not have to go home for lunch (as I did, nearly every Sunday) afterwards. How could I ever explain this to my parents, let alone my friends? That evening I put on my best suit and made my way into the little village church, near where I lived. I just hoped that no-one would speak to me. I wanted to give the impression to all there that I was a seasoned churchgoer. They must not know that I could not find my way around the prayer book.

Once in the pew my apprehension and self-consciousness erupted in the form of a heavy sweat. How embarrassed I was! I managed the prayer book fairly well, although once or twice when I was a little lost, the woman next to me smiled and showed me the place. I was not aware of fumbling for long enough to make her suspicious, but my newness to this environment must have shown. I wanted to rush out as inconspicuously as possible, hoping that no-one would say anything to me. There were about twenty-five people in the neat and fairly plain old church building and they all seemed to know each other. The vicar was busy talking to people as they left. He glanced over to me and looked as if he would rush towards me through the people around him, if I lingered at all. I made him be content with a glance at me and the words, 'Nice to see you here!' I nodded and beat a hasty retreat.

I later told Tim that I had been to church, although without admitting the difficulties involved in the process. He began to ask if it was a church where the gospel was preached and then explained what he meant by that. He told me how he had become a Christian while at school. I had heard in our own school chapel, years previously, that Christ died for our sins, though what that actually meant had never been formalised or worked out in my brain: it was just words. As Tim gently shared his own experiences with me, it all made so much more sense than ever before. The idea of sin separating me from God, and Jesus as the perfect sacrifice for that sin, was something I could begin to understand and accept, rather than the complex phraseology of the formal prayers in school. Underlining this new found understanding of the gospel was the fact that I was beginning to understand something of the perfect humanity of Jesus, through reading Matthew's Gospel. The personality that really shone through the pages to me was one of a perfect man. He seemed to lack any fear, prejudice, anger or other human traits that I had assumed were quite normal. These very special qualities of Jesus made me realise that he really is God and also encouraged me to pay very close attention to all that he was teaching through the Gospel account.

I found that the inner voice that spoke to me on that journey home from Chester, was now a constant companion. Sometimes in the bakery I would experience God's presence in unexpected ways. For example, my hand would pull away seconds before some boiling jam was spilt. It could not have been a reflex action because it happened before the jam spilt, not at the same time, or after. On other occasions I would be packing some fancy cakes and pick up a handful of cases for them. Many, many times there were exactly the right amount – no more no less. On all these occasions the inner voice just gently said, 'You see it's going to be all right, everything will work out' and each time I felt a sense of real assurance and peace. Tim had left a booklet with me called *Journey Into Life*. This was a simple and straightforward account of the gospel and how to become a Christian. It was well illustrated with helpful diagrams and ended with the prayer of commitment. It seemed to relate very much to all that I had been experiencing of God and had learned from Tim. I thought I had made a decision in my spirit, to follow Christ, when on the way home from Chester, but prayed the prayer of commitment in the book just to be doubly sure. I continued to go to the local church and although the vicar did sometimes mention something of a personal relationship with Christ, rather than the religious intellectualism I heard before, he seemed a bit vague and disillusioned. In almost every sermon he asked us to consider giving more money towards church repairs. I sensed very much that he was fighting a lonely battle. Tim phoned one day to say that he had arranged to see a vicar near Birkenhead, called Roy Barker. 'I have prayed that God will speak to me through him, on this whole question of my homosexuality. Will you pray for me too?' I agreed, with some apprehension.

'How did you get on Tim?' I said, when he phoned a couple of hours later.

'Very well. I'm sure our prayers were answered. Roy really seemed to understand what I was talking about. He has come across it before. He said, "Tim, I know some people will tell you differently, but I'm sorry I feel I have to say that Scripture clearly says homosexual practice is wrong. It doesn't condemn you for having a homosexual orientation and temptations." ' Tim continued, 'He showed me where this is mentioned in Scripture and I do feel at peace about it now. I am sure he is right, you know. You and I prayed that God would speak through him and I feel that has happened.'

'I'm not sure, Tim,' I said. 'Why should God say it's wrong?'

'Because God intends sex only within marriage.'

'But why should we have these feelings if they're not right?' I asked.

'I don't know, but I do believe that God can give me the power to overcome them and maybe even take them away. I'd love to be able to get married and have a family, one day.'

'Well, I guess he might be right,' I said rather unconvinced.

'I really must start going to his church,' Tim said, 'I've heard quite a bit about it. Perhaps you could come over one Sunday?'

I agreed. I knew in my heart that what he was saying was right. Having read Matthew's Gospel I found it difficult to believe that Jesus would condone homosexual relationships. It just seemed so inconsistent with the rest of his moral teaching. Needless to say, I was a bit reluctant to admit this change of attitude to Tim, because it seemed such an 'about-turn' remembering my efforts to persuade him to accept the homosexual lifestyle! Eventually, at a later meeting, I admitted to him that what Roy had said really did make sense.

At this time I did not experience a strong desire to pick someone up for sex. My mind was too preoccupied with other things. In the past, I had usually managed to remain faithful to my 'lovers' and stop all promiscuous sexual activity. However, there were now times when I would

pass a familiar place and almost stop the car from sheer
force of habit. Each time this happened a voice within
screamed, 'No!' Thoughts of losing all the ground I had
gained, especially in my relationship with Tim, came
flooding in and I was too fearful to give in to temptation.

A few weeks later, Tim took me to Upton St Mary's,
Roy Barker's church, and I was impressed by so much
there. Firstly, it was full. I had no idea that any churches
attracted this many people! The general atmosphere was
bright and friendly and the order of service was easy to
follow, just a slip of paper in the back of the psalter. Even
I could not feel embarrassed. There was a little informality
in the service. You did not feel that a note or cough out of
place, maybe even a few words, would cause a stir to the
congregation. It was even a surprise to hear Roy actually
say, 'Good evening' at the start of the service and more of
a surprise to hear the congregation reply. However, what
impressed me more than anything else was the way in
which the people there were talking together about what
the Lord was doing in their lives. We could pick up little
snippets of conversation as we waited in the long queue to
leave the church building. I could identify with them and
what they were saying. This made me feel at home more
than anything else. Roy himself was a stockily built
middle-aged man, with slightly thinning dark brown hair.
I was especially struck by his homely nature and gentle
fatherly wisdom. His Yorkshire inflection and sense of
humour were charming. 'I could probably relate to him,
without feeling too daunted' I thought.

Roy held a 'Vicar's Hour' on a Thursday evening, a bit
like a doctor's surgery, and I began to go over to see him as
often as possible. Thursday came and I made the forty
minute journey to Upton. On the first occasion I was a
little late for the start of Vicar's Hour and a bit unsure of

which door to use. I saw one or two people outside the vestry door of the church and guessed that must be the right one. I stayed in the car, trying to pluck up the courage to go in. Eventually it was too late – or at least I assumed it was because of the time. I returned home feeling defeated and depressed.

The next week, I managed to see Roy and, like Tim, was struck by his warmth, friendliness and knowledge of the subject. He seemed delighted at what had happened in my life and said, 'Who knows what the Lord has for you to do? Perhaps even overseas missionary work!' He said it would always be nice to see me at St Mary's, but felt really a more local church would be better. He made a point of saying how important it was for me to become involved in the local church. He mentioned a few possibilities in the Liverpool area.

I was worried Roy might attempt to dissuade me from continuing the relationship with Tim, although I was prepared for this. However, he did not do this which encouraged me. Meanwhile I still continued to go to the pubs and clubs, as did Tim. A few of my friends knew something of what was happening in my life, although they were obviously suspicious that it was in order to please Tim, rather than anything else.

I tried various churches in Liverpool and became something of a 'spiritual gypsy' but nothing really compared with what I had experienced in Upton. I was very conscious of not appearing to be following Tim or putting too much pressure on him. I therefore sought to 'do my own thing', in terms of churchgoing, to establish my own Christian identity. There was always the thought in the back of my mind that I might be doing all this to keep Tim's friendship. Was my love for the Lord really more important to me than Tim?

Then, all of a sudden Tim's job moved him to London. In some ways I was sad about this; in other ways relieved. It meant the pressure of deciding to see him or not was no longer there, and I would be able to continue my Christian experience without wondering about what he was thinking and how often I could see him. It would also help to prove my sincerity to my friends. My mother and father knew that I had started going to church and said they were pleased about this. At first they compared it with my brother's experience, but I think I soon convinced them that it was very different. I also began to go to Upton far more frequently and saw Roy about the possibility of being confirmed. I was blissfully naïve and unaware of denominations at that stage. I still saw the Church as the traditional Church of England with a spire, bells and robes. Confirmation seemed necessary for me to affirm publicly that I had decided to follow Christ. Certainly my journey to that point of decision had been very unorthodox. All I could say was that God knew my vulnerable spot and used that to bring his love into my life.

Jesus told Nicodemus 'I tell you the truth, unless a man is born again, he cannot see the Kingdom of God' (John 3.3). I was beginning to appreciate the reality of that in my own life, but I found so many feelings and attitudes in my life changing, before I understood the meaning of being 're-born'. It seemed that God was at work in my life before explaining to me what he was doing!

4: A Child in Christ

As I read and understood more Scripture, I found my new faith and experience made a lot of sense. A real thirst for God's word was there, despite the fact that for so many years reading books had not been one of my pastimes. My zeal to learn more helped me to concentrate, although my memory, especially for names, facts and figures still leaves a lot to be desired! There were times when old insecurities re-surfaced, but I was aware of Jesus' presence in such a very real way that they were soon overcome. For example, I remember being with Tim in a club, before he went to London and suddenly being overcome by a fear of losing him. The next moment I felt Jesus put his arms around me and I knew comfort, assurance and peace. Nowadays it would probably be thought of as a type of 'prayer imagination'. I did not work out the theological or spiritual implications at the time. I knew Jesus was with me, so why not use my imagination to experience the reality of his presence?

As I became more involved at the church in Upton, so Christian fellowship became increasingly important to me. I wanted to share what God was doing in my life and hear more about him through others. There was a wonderful new freedom in not wanting to hide or pretend to be someone I was not. This also changed my attitude at work. They were a bit taken aback by the change in me. The swearing and the blaspheming had obviously stopped and I was getting used to the looks of amazement when I refused to 'rise to the bait' and respond in my old way to their jokes and comments. A few remarks like, 'We'll have to watch ourselves with holy Joe around!' were made, but on the whole there seemed to be a quiet respect. I had found a new ally in our manageress, who was a Christian. She was respected by nearly all the staff, although sometimes joked about. I now had more respect for her than ever before. She had been with us many years before I was born and, despite our being situated in a tough, 'red light' district of Liverpool she still blushed if anyone swore or used obscene language, usually pretending not to hear. Sadly, in some ways, my Christianity made me feel a loss of identity with the other bakehouse workers, because our lifestyles were now even more different than before. At least I no longer felt I had to convince them I was a womaniser! Even though I did not want my bakehouse friends to know about my homosexual past, my freedom from gay involvement made me feel I was no longer hiding anything. Witnessing was something my church fellowship encouraged and occasionally I overcame my reserve and shared my new-found faith with others. I nervously tuned the bakehouse radio into 'Prayer for the Day', 'Thought for the Day' and 'Pause for Thought' – sometimes even the morning service. The volume was gingerly raised, unless the talk was not Bible-based or evangelical, in which case I rapidly turned it down! I felt the Lord had carefully placed my workbench underneath the radio shelf for a specific purpose. There were a few complaints, but normally just a rather embarrassed silence. I was very conscious that they must see the 'change' in me and therefore refused to lose my temper.

Nowadays I wonder how much of a real human being they saw in me!

Another area of freedom and a sense of purity I experienced was in finding myself in parts of Liverpool where in the past I would have looked for sexual contacts. Before, I would have worked out a series of excuses for being there, just in case the police or anyone I knew came by. Now, because I no longer had the same motivations and desires, my defences were not necessary. It felt good to be innocent. This also applied to my car, which had been renewed since I became a Christian. It is possible that the police knew of my other car, as I think the vice squad made a note of cars seen around notorious homosexual pick-up points, but I knew for certain that my new car would not be on their records.

The Lord had also given me a new desire to help other people. A way of fulfilling this need, it seemed, could be through working for a voluntary counselling organisation, so I joined the Samaritans. This is not a Christian organisation as such but was the only one I knew which took voluntary help (I should explain that there is a rule that no volunteer is to declare himself or herself; but I have not been involved with them for over eight years now). The preparation course was very helpful and interesting, although I was nervous at times and daunted by the prospect of the work. When I began work I made continual cries to the Lord for help and strength to cope, which he supplied.

I remember one occasion when I was the only male on duty in the centre when a very drunk and angry man was banging on the door and demanding to be let in. Arrow prayers were going up thick and fast as I made my way towards him. It seemed quite likely from his mood that he would attack me – we could see him through the window even punching his own shadow! When I eventually opened the door and met him face to face I suddenly felt a tremendous love for him and to my amazement (as a 'number one coward') fear evaporated and the expression on his face transformed. I saw warmth, love and gentleness in his eyes. I was able to reason with him and help him on his way. Although we were not supposed to talk about our faith the leaders knew my reason for joining was a Christian commitment, and I soon found God provided me with opportunies to witness. Needless to say I quite often failed to make the most of them. I soon felt convicted about this and prayed that God would give me more opportunities. I was amazed how they were provided, without any need to break the rules. For example, a client would ask, 'I don't know if you're religious, but would you please pray for me'! Often I would be asked for my opinion by a client and having explained the rules that we can only 'suggest' not 'advise', would be given permission to share my belief and faith. I obviously made it very clear that it was my own Christian belief, not the view or policy of the organisation.

This work was to prepare me in many ways for the future, but one of the greatest things I gained from it was an understanding and love for my own brother. I heard about and met so many people with similar personality and psychological problems that I no longer saw evil in him, but the hurt and trauma of a complex personality problem. I still found it difficult to relate to him, but it was now in a completely different way. A love for him was there, even though feebly expressed.

At this time I was still seeing something of my old friends and occasionally had a meal with them. I was beginning to find these social evenings a bit difficult because of a strong internal conflict. I desperately wanted them to see the change God had brought to my life, so that they would seek him themselves. They would chat with me in the same way as in the past. However, I now not only had nothing to give to the conversation, as far as sex, boyfriends and other interests were concerned, but often felt offended by their language and jokes. This really hurt me because I knew my language and crude, blasphemous sense of humour used to be far worse than theirs. I think they sensed my uneasiness, which caused some tension in the atmosphere. In some ways I was almost scared to be 'me' and felt I had to come over as a new and different person, a radiant and transformed Christian without any problems or difficulties. It was much later that God showed me how his love and the way of Christ is not as simple and painless as that. Many years afterwards, a close homosexual friend made a remark which meant a lot to me. He said, 'Dear Martin you haven't changed – you're still as dizzy as ever!' If he had said that during the early part of my Christian life, I would have been really dismayed. I was so conscious of the need to appear to be totally transformed.

Many of my friends were still staying overnight, when they visited me and they would sleep together. At first I thought nothing of this, but I began to feel that it was not honouring to the Lord for me to say that homosexual sex is wrong and then allow it possibly to take place in my own house. It seemed I would have to say something to them – but how? I was horrified at what I thought their reaction might be. It could appear that I was rejecting them. They would have every right to tell me to get lost – to disown me. I phoned Dave, my closest friend and the one who seemed the most sympathetic to my Christian commitment. I began, 'Dave . . . I think there is something

I need to say to you and the others but . . . Oh boy, it's so difficult – you've got every right to tell me to get lost . . . ' Eventually, I was able to explain what I thought and why. To my amazement he said, 'Martin, don't worry about it, I understand. There's no need to mention it again. If you like I can tell the others. It won't make any difference, don't worry. It's great to see you so happy, but I don't think it's for me.' I was overjoyed that the Lord had prepared his heart so wonderfully. I told the others myself and they were equally understanding.

In fact I was especially humbled by Ken's reaction. He has since moved back to London to be near his beloved Covent Garden and set up home with a male lover. Ken wanted his new friend to visit Liverpool and especially to meet me! He said, 'Martin, please don't be offended, but could you find us an hotel to stay in, because we know and respect your feelings? We don't want you to be hurt or embarrassed in any way.' I was horrified to think of Ken and his friend staying in an hotel, rather than with me and told him so. He then said, 'Well perhaps we could sleep in separate rooms?' I was embarrassed and wondered if it was right for me to take such a firm stand. Ken sensed this, 'Don't say another word Martin. That's settled, we will stay with you.' They did and we had great fun together.

In his book, *Knowing God*, James Packer shares how the Lord often encourages new Christians with 'little sweeties' of experience. Then may come the time when they must rely on faith alone to sustain them through difficult times. Well, I was still a 'babe' in Christ and the Lord was constantly making me aware of his love and presence, and at that stage it must still have been necessary to have 'little sweeties'. It was easy to be tempted to doubt the validity of all that God was doing and return to my old way of life, although this seemed an impossible thought at the time.

Working from an early morning start in the bakehouse had often led to overtiredness. Frequently, when driving home late at night I was aware of falling asleep at the wheel of the car. Thankfully, a jolt by the kerb would wake me enough to continue. However, one night I was travelling from Ormskirk to my home on the outskirts of Liverpool down winding, unlit roads. I was only too aware of falling asleep at the wheel and asked the Lord to help me. I know the sensible step is always to pull over for a snooze, but I did not want to do this, probably because it would make me even later for bed at home, with even less time before I was up at 4.45 am. I am convinced that I fell asleep at the wheel that night. I cannot remember anything from drifting into sleep whilst driving down a country road, to waking up with a start and suddenly slamming on my brakes – in my drive, at home! I had motored down a lane, turned into the large open-plan housing estate with identical houses and found my house and drive, whilst still unconscious! My first reaction when I woke up was that the Lord had driven me home and I thanked him. When I told my non-Christian friends they were not impressed, saying, 'You can do things automatically.' I replied, 'Sure, but not if your eyes are closed!' It was several years later that I heard about angels. Psalm 91.11 says, 'For he will command his angels concerning you to guard you in all your ways; they will lift you up in their hands, so that you will not strike your foot against a stone.' This made a lot of sense to me and I realised that angels had protected me then and on several occasions before and since.

As I read more of God's word, the Lord not only seemed to speak to my everyday situation, but also showed me how much his pattern for our lives made sense. As I learned more, I longed to share it with others, especially Tim, now in London. Sadly he often felt threatened by this and sometimes thought I was 'getting at him'. I was too insensitive and clumsy to realise this – in fact I know now that often I *was* trying to 'get at him'! I worried about the fact he was not making identical spiritual progress to myself and could always see the possibility of his deeper involvement in the gay lifestyle. London was certainly the most likely place in the country for this to happen. Tim was very attractive, both in looks and personality, and often seemed to get into difficult situations. Someone would make it clear that they were attracted to him and smile or glance his way. He would sometimes feel honour-bound to respond, which often caused problems with temptation. We already had a small circle of homosexual friends in London, but Tim had no regular church commitment.

Meanwhile the only Christian fellowship I had was through my visits to Upton, for church meetings and Sunday services. The regular confirmation classes were a great encouragement for me, as we talked and shared our faith together under Roy Barker's leadership. He explained so many ways of applying one's faith and shared a lot of his personal testimony. Roy also did everything possible to make sure that Christians were exercising a ministry. His phone calls – 'I've got a little job I thought you might like to do . . . ' – were notorious. It is so important that Christians are able to feel they are doing something for the Lord. I believe God created that need within us. Roy encouraged me to go out with one of his lay ministers, who used to visit and have some pastoral responsibility for areas of the parish. This certainly helped me to overcome some of my shyness and encouraged me to share my faith. It was also very interesting to sit in on the lay ministers' meetings, as they shared about their own experiences of visiting. Why was I chosen to be involved in this, when I had only been a Christian a relatively short time (not much more than a year) and was so shy? There is no doubt that Roy's God-given wisdom had seen this as the best way forward for me and, as usual, Roy had thrown convention to the wind.

The confirmation was a wonderful event for me, with my father, mother and brother all attending, plus some Christian aunts, uncles and cousins – the ones I used to keep at arm's length and find a bit strange, but now could identify with in a new way. Tim did say he would try to make my confirmation, but could not promise. Before the service there was no sign of him and I assumed he was not there. Then, as I stood up and turned around after the Bishop laid hands on me, the first person I saw in the congregation was Tim. Our eyes met and we smiled. I thought it was a wonderful touch of God's love.

Now that the commitment of the confirmation classes was over, my midweek visits to Upton were a little less frequent. I had not made any really close friends over there, but at that stage did not seem too concerned. I was still discovering so much that was exciting in my relationship with Jesus, everything else seemed less important. I even gave away my two Burmese cats, to whom I was devoted. 'I don't need them now,' I said, 'I've got the Lord Jesus.'

Then, after one Sunday evening service at Upton St Mary's, I had an experience that seemed so strange, that for years I hesitated to share it. At the end of the service I noticed a whole row of figure eights at the top of the hymn text we had just sung. Then I glanced at the noticeboard, which said 'Eighth after Trinity'. I had never attached any importance to numbers before. On the way home I found myself compulsively noting numbers on road signs or car licence plates. The number eight kept reappearing. Even if I added numbers together it always made eight. In no way do I have a mathematical brain, but every time I added two of the numbers I saw together, it came to eight! For example the motorway home was the M53 (5 + 3 = 8). I then started to think of dates and add them together. The same thing happened, yet as I said before, my brain does not function well enough to know beforehand the end product of any numbers I add. 'The date of my confirmation was September 26th (2 + 6 = 8). My birthday is the 14th March (3rd month – 1 + 4 + 3 = 8). And so it went on. I kept telling myself, 'Stop . . . this is ridiculous!'

When I arrived home I opened the Bible Tim had given me and noticed the text in the front. It read, 'Jesus said, "If you continue in my word, you are truly my disciples, and you will know the truth, and the truth will make you free" ' (John 8.31, 32). 'Funny "eight" again,' I thought. I felt a bit stupid and doubted really that it meant anything. Was I going slightly mad?

The next morning at 4.45 I was in my usual semi-conscious state, about to put the kettle on for a morning 'fix' of coffee to waken me, when I noticed a red admiral butterfly flapping helplessly around the small kitchen. 'How odd,' I thought. Firstly butterflies had been very scarce that year and secondly I had never known one to be trapped indoors like that. Moths yes, frequently, but never butterflies. In my still somewhat dozy state I carefully manoeuvred it towards the window, which I opened to release it into the fresh air. As it made for freedom the Lord said, 'You've set it free. You will be setting others free.' I was stunned. There are times when you wonder if that inner voice is really the Lord.

Sometimes, the words are so meaningful and detached from any conscious thought or idea that you have had. Then you can feel certain that the voice is not your imagination at all. This was such an occasion. For the rest of that day I was still in a fairly dazed state. By the next day I had recovered. I thought 'Another of those experiences!' That Wednesday I decided to go to the midweek church meeting. I had not been for several weeks. The person leading the Bible study started to speak, 'Tonight we are going to look at John chapter eight.' I was stunned, yet again. As I looked around the open Bibles before me, the pages almost seemed to be glowing with a brilliant white, like the washing powder adverts. I must have been very moved because I stood up and shared, without going into every detail (I was too embarrassed), what I felt the Lord had been saying. I was still puzzled, not really knowing what it all meant. Many years later, it became clear.

The family business was due to be closed down because of a compulsory purchase order. I had no great interest in the business and thought, with my Samaritan experience behind me, I would like to do some sort of social work. However, it was all a bit uncertain, and it seemed logical for me to think about moving to Upton because there was only a small mortgage on my house in Liverpool and a cheaper one could be bought in Upton to clear it. I was very fond of my Liverpool home, but the advantages of being within easy walking distance of the church, rather than forty minutes away by car, clinched it. I moved and my parents bought my house to use for their retirement. It all worked out very well indeed. For a while, until we finally closed the bakery, I commuted to work from Upton. We had a farewell party in my house and I will never forget the ordeal of simply sharing a few words with the staff before we made some presentations. It gives an indication of just how shy I was to say that, even with people I knew in my own home, speaking to an audience was very traumatic – the sweat poured off me.

Once settled into my new home it was really good to be nearer church. However, it was not quite as I had imagined. People did not just pop in, unless invited. I still felt quite lonely and most of my friends were married. I began to get more involved with a group of mainly single people, called Senior CYFA. A curate from the church, John, was always very warm and loving to me and we were beginning to get to know one another. He was tall and slim with immaculately groomed long black hair and beard. Many people remarked that he looked like Jesus!

Before the bakery finally closed and I was on the dole, I decided to have a little party to which I would invite my closest homosexual friends and some of the Christians I knew at church. The motive behind this was to witness to my friends and help them to see what had been happening in my life. The Christians were from many different social, academic and even denominational backgrounds. Most of them had led a fairly 'sheltered' life, but were apparently almost unshockable. Having originally told them that I was inviting some of my non-Christian friends, it suddenly dawned on me that though they all knew about my own homosexual background they may not realise that all these friends would also be homosexual. I hastily phoned round and said, 'I think you ought to know . . . Well, all of my friends coming are homosexual!' A typical response was simply, 'Fine Martin. What time did you say you wanted us to arrive?' As far as my homosexual friends were concerned, I am sure they felt it was a bit like 'throwing the pagans into the Christian Lion's Den'. John had a good chat with one man from

Manchester and came into the kitchen, obviously greatly encouraged. 'He asked if we could go and spend the weekend with him. Is that OK with you?' I agreed, then about half an hour later a somewhat crestfallen John said to me, 'I think we'd better call off the weekend. I think he's got the wrong idea! I so much want to tell him I love him but I'm scared that it might be misinterpreted!' It seemed he had been gently propositioned! At one stage a Christian woman went up to another friend of mine, gazed into his handsome face and said, 'You're not like the others, are you? You're not homosexual?' There was a very embarrassed reply, 'Well . . . er . . . . Yes I am!'

'But you can't be!' she gasped, 'I know girls who would queue from here down the street for a date with you!' One of my friends did get slightly drunk and I was concerned that a strictly teetotal, non-smoking, no television, elderly Christian lady and prayer warrior would have been offended. When asked, she replied, 'Oh no Martin, I believe the Lord used the alcohol to loosen his tongue!' It was certainly an unusual evening, but I doubted its success in the way I had envisaged it.

Before long Roy Barker organised a 'consultation at the vicarage' for anyone wishing to meet up with someone whom Christ had brought out of homosexuality. It was mentioned in the church magazine and it was not long before the local 'gay group' heard about it. They contacted him to ask if they could send some representatives. Roy thought it was a great idea. They were 'nibbling at his bait'. It was a very intimate meeting with the two homosexuals and five Christians. I knew the men from the gay group quite well and they were really taken aback to see me there. In my enthusiasm I talked about 'victory', 'bondage' and used other evangelical terminology, which had become so much a part of my vocabulary. As might be expected they took offence at the use of these words and were verbally aggressive and abusive. It seemed they were under the impression they had been invited to talk to *us* about homosexuality! Roy graciously pointed out that this was not quite the way it had been intended. Eventually they stopped protesting and one of them said, 'Maybe we ought to know more about this Jesus you are all talking about!' Roy moved in quickly, 'But you can . . . ' and they did.

One evening I gave my testimony at an after church meeting in my home. I had decided, after talking it through with one or two others, that I should be perfectly open about my way of life and not be concerned about shocking them too much. So I was perfectly open and afterwards it seemed as if I had been talking about a Sunday school outing – there was no obvious shock expressed at all. Any event like this usually filled me with horror because of my shyness, becoming a mighty event on my calendar which I worried about for days or weeks ahead; but on this occasion I was quite at ease.

Soon we were using my house for the young people's meetings. We called it 'Senior CYFA' and some of us were a lot more 'senior' than others! My relationship with John and the other curate Mark, developed and we became friends, although there were the sort of limits on the relationships one would expect at this stage, with a curate and parishioner. I still felt something of a loner and wondered if there could really be anyone else like me, from a homosexual background. I also became very conscious of the way in which churches divide people into groupings: 'Marrieds', 'Singles', 'Old Wives', 'Young Wives', 'Youth Groups', 'Pensioners', and so on. I found it difficult to understand and appreciate because amongst my homosexual friends those barriers were not there. I understood the special situations and experiences that each of those groups needed to share with one another, but I found it difficult to see why they were all really necessary.

5: Love Hurts

After a couple of weeks on the dole, the bakery having closed in 1974, Roy Barker offered me a job as the Church Hallkeeper. This was caretaking work, opening and closing the hall for various organisations and keeping it clean. It meant I had to be on call many times during the day and evening, but with lots of spare time. Roy, John and I wondered if the Lord could be calling me into the ordained ministry and this was a good time to explore that idea.

My relationship with John was deepening, but in keeping with many of my other relationships it was rather superficial. This was probably because with both men and women I always tended to wait for the other person to make the first move of friendship towards me. There was always a nagging doubt thtat they would reject me. There may have been an element of fear on their part, because of my background and, perhaps, their inability to identify with my past and present situation. It was many years before I learned to recognise this fear in many of my friends.

The Bible tells us that 'We love God because he first loved us,' (1 John 4.19). My love for God and dependence on him were now increasing as he revealed more and more of his love to me. Also John's warm, loving and sensitive nature really attracted me. He seemed a vulnerable person, but with a strong, striking personality, and his loving concern and charisma attracted a lot of people to him. I found a deep love developing, but did not feel shame about it. I shared my feelings with him, telling him there was nothing required in return, and found I could love in an exciting new way, in accordance with Scripture. For a while John's relationship with me was not much deeper than that which he shared with many others in our Senior CYFA group. To my amazement I felt quite content with this, provided I was allowed to love, and I made an effort not to put any pressure on him.

Then one weekend we were all away at a houseparty and it became pretty clear that John was very depressed. He shared the great burden on his heart, which involved a difficult relationship with a girl in the parish. It has been said that one of the greatest gifts of love is self-disclosure. If we are prepared to share something with someone we are saying, 'I am trusting you.' John's gift of love to me meant a lot, and I was apparently one of the very few people who knew his secret. He eventually said that it was going to be very difficult for him to prepare his sermon. For John preparation usually meant many hours of sweat and toil, with copious notes but on this occasion he could not get down to it. Then, again taking me into his confidence he said that he felt he should share his testimony.

It was one of the most moving sermons I have ever heard. Many times John almost broke down in the pulpit as he shared his life with us. Then he told us in a tremendously humble way how much being a popular charismatic leader had done for his ego. 'If you follow me you'll be in a mess,' he said, 'because I'm in a mess – but if you follow Jesus his strength will be made perfect through weakness.' His text was 'We have this treasure in earthen vessels,' (2 Cor. 4.7).

At the end, Roy stood up and thanked John for all he had shared. He added, 'If he thinks he is weak, then I am ten times weaker.' John had requested as a final hymn 'Peace, Perfect Peace in This Dark World of Sin', but very few of us could sing we were so choked with emotion. I was, as usual, not able to express my emotions during the service, but afterwards, as I listened to the recording, I wept. I shared in the pain he was expressing, as my relationship with John and his girlfriend meant so much to me. The two of them often invited me to join them at the cinema, or they simply popped in for a quiet evening. If I ever made noises about being a 'gooseberry' I was just told to be quiet. John frequently called in late at night, when we would sit and natter, or just relax with music, for hours. Then at, perhaps 2.00 am we would decide to make some porridge! It was crazy, but wonderful.

I often felt depressed and condemned when my shyness had prevented me from praying out loud at meetings. John used to give me a very 'knowing' and loving look and silently mouth, 'Are you all right?' I often felt embarrassed on these occasions, wondering what on earth people would be thinking. Would they think *he* was homosexual? However, it meant so much to know that he was prepared to show his love without concern for what others might think. He was prepared to be seen as a friend of mine. Does that not remind you of Jesus' love – 'the friend of tax collectors and sinners'? It was a new experience for me to be loving two people as much as Tim and John, without feeling threatened or insecure. Jealousy and possessiveness did not seem to be a problem. Without feeling like some kind of masochistic martyr I felt I could give in a way which brought positive purpose to these relationships.

David Watson once said, 'Love that cost nothing is worth what it costs – nothing'. However, I tended not to move towards other people in our group and relate on such a deep level with them as I did with John. I wanted to protect John and his girlfriend's privacy, the fact they felt it necessary to keep their relationship secret. I doubt that this prevented any other possible relationships developing for me. If it did, it was a cost very gladly borne, as I learnt more from John at this time than any other person.

When someone you love very much is hurting, then of course you are hurting with them. Often there is a sense of real helplessness when you feel there is nothing you can do, because it might put too much pressure on the person concerned. With John and Tim it seemed that their crises rarely coincided, but once they did. I remember crying helplessly to God, 'Oh Lord, why do I love them so much?' Immediately, came the reply, 'Because I do.' It was an instant response to my question: it must be from the Lord. I could never have thought of anything as profound yet simple, so quickly! As I thought about these words, they encouraged me yet again to continue on this road of costly loving. I have needed to learn the lesson over and over again. I was beginning to know something of the qualities of love in 1 Corinthians 13, but there was (and is) a long way to go down that path. In many ways I was far too arrogant in thinking I was pretty good at selfless loving!

I was able to meet Tim's family. That is, those who were Christians; his sister, brother-in-law, and sister-in-law. He was very much on edge in case they found out about his homosexuality, although deep down, he still thought his sister and her husband, Jane and Andrew, ought to know. I spent a few days with the family in the Lake District. It was a wonderful new experience for me.

We walked through the beautiful scenery and would sometimes just stop and thank the Lord for the marvel of his creation. With all these new influences I began to see how much I had missed in my late teens and early twenties. Life had been so sex-orientated that other hobbies, interests and sports were ignored. Tim and his family had been into horse riding and various other activities. I envied them and really felt I had missed out. Music was also something Christians seemed to be quite good at. Many played the guitar and piano. Was it too late for me to start, at thirty?

My relationships with women have always been good, but never reached a deep level. Men with homosexual feelings often relate well to women, even though there may be no strong emotional and sexual attraction. I still found it difficult to identify with Tim's desire to settle down and have a family. There were quite a few women at church with whom I really felt at home and I enjoyed being with them, but could not envisage marriage in any way. In St Mary's it was becoming increasingly clear how much emotional trauma so many single Christian women face. I found it gave me a great feeling of empathy with them, but made me a bit wary, just in case any had problems concerning me. That, however, was very rare indeed! Either the women were not interested in me, or just felt I was a 'hopeless case'.

It was a great joy to use my home for hospitality to visiting speakers and sometimes Christian musicians, dancers and actors. I guess the latter revitalised my old interests in theatre. I was greatly blessed to meet some of the Swedish choir, 'Choralerna' and to get to know them. When I knew they were also visiting London I wanted Tim to meet them, as I believed that the Lord was directing me to lead Tim into a church fellowship. He still had not settled in one and, although he always intended to do something about it, nothing was done! In my usual approach, as sensitive as a 'sledge-hammer', I determined to go down to London for the weekend, to impress Tim with Choralerna and find him a church. I made enquiries and a suitable church was found.

In the meantime Tim had become very friendly with a dancer called Michael, who was homosexual. Tim had told him about God and said he wondered if the Lord would move in Michael's life as he had in mine. I met Michael that weekend and it soon became obvious that he was very much in love with Tim. Many feelings and emotions were whirling inside me, as it seemed like a dangerous situation. Michael was a very nice person, but had not responded to the gospel at all. I felt he was living in hope of having a homosexual relationship with Tim and that frightened me. Where could the relationship go from here? It could only hurt Michael or possibly drag Tim into a homosexual relationship, from which he might not have the will, power or desire to escape. Where was the Lord in all this? I believed I had to persuade Tim to break off the relationship, but was aware that he would think it was more of a jealous tantrum on my part, than the Lord.

After a lot of soul-searching and heartache prayer, I felt I knew what I had to say to him. I shared, as honestly as I could, what I was feeling. Then I said in order to prove to myself and to him that my motives were right, that I was prepared to end our own relationship, once he had finished with Michael and settled in a church fellowship. It did not seem right for me to let go completely until he was in a fellowship. Tim seemed a bit reluctant, feeling that Michael might still come to the Lord. He agreed to come with me to the local church I had found. During the last hymn, Tim suddenly broke down. I was stunned and felt helpless, I longed to put my arms around him and comfort him, but felt too shy, though I made a feeble attempt to do so. He eventually composed himself and left having chatted briefly to the vicar who had obviously seen his distress and wanted to help. Once in the car, he broke down again and sobbed, realising that I was right and he must end the relationship with Michael. Then it was my turn to start sobbing uncontrollably. I had no idea he had felt so strongly about Michael and it now seemed as if I had been responsible for hurting Tim. I not only shared his hurt, but felt that I had caused it. We just lovingly ministered to one another. Tim said, 'You know I really didn't want you to come down this weekend, but now I don't want you to go'.

Later that evening, when I had arrived home, Tim phoned. 'Something amazing has happened,' he said. 'I called in to see Jane and Andrew and Jane said, "What's the matter Tim?" and I broke down. She said, "Is it a girl? . . . Is it a man?" Martin, I have been able to share everything with her and Andrew. They were marvellous!' I was really able to share in his joy. He said that he would see Michael the next day and explain everything. We both prayed and agreed that the Lord would prepare that situation as he had done everything else: he did. Michael agreed with Tim that it was hopeless, to continue together and Tim 'gave' Michael to the Lord as an act of love and submission.

As far as my possible ordination was concerned, a selection conference was arranged and I went in great fear and trembling. It was thrilling to see the Lord overrule and give me so much strength and confidence. I was certain I must have been accepted, but they turned me down on the grounds I may not be able to cope with the academic work required in training. It really hurt: was God playing games with me? To give me the confidence and assurance, only to take it away. I felt hurt, only this time by God.

Roy Barker was a marvellous encouragement, of course, and having consulted with the Director of Ordinands, felt it right that I should take some 'O' levels to prove that I could cope with the academic work necessary to train for the ministry. Eventually, it was felt I should probably apply again, and I continued working at the Church Hall, while getting two 'O' levels.

One night at eleven I had a phone call from the hospital to say that my mother, who had a heart condition had been admitted and was in intensive care. I phoned John to ask him to pray. Despite being thoroughly exhausted (I had only just driven him home, because he was too tired to drive) he insisted on coming over to the hospital in Liverpool with me. This obviously meant a lot to me and my father. Mother died that night, but we could all see God's hand in the situation very clearly. God proved to be Lord of life and death as well as comforter. John took the funeral, which was a wonderful witness of God's goodness and faithfulness. I was still unable to cry. The responsibility for organising the funeral and sharing the news with relatives and friends was mine. I felt God's enabling so much at this time, but in some ways it was as if it was all not really happening. At least I no longer found funerals quite as strange as in the past, because I was now helping with them at church. I found at this time that although God had blessed me with various gifts of the Spirit I still found it difficult to cry openly. The Holy Spirit still had a lot of work to do with my emotions.

On the whole I felt pretty good about all that God had

been doing in my life, but I had real difficulty identifying or even sympathising with Christians struggling with problems I felt I no longer had. Then I suddenly became aware of homosexual feelings and temptations. It shook me; after four years as a Christian, how could this happen to me? I shared my feelings with John, who was probably surprised that I should make such an issue of it. My emotions had been rocked a bit. Now I found I could identify with many of the people I had possibly even hurt by my lack of real understanding. The words of the Apostle Paul about his 'thorn in the flesh' (2 Cor. 12.7) had a whole new meaning for me.

Then John moved to Liverpool. The late night porridge and chats had gone, and I began to feel lonely and sometimes even unloved. Lies from the enemy maybe, but the 'little sweeties' from the Lord were being replaced by more solid food. I was starting to appreciate something new about the 'treasure' Paul talks about in my 'jar of clay' (2 Cor. 4.7).

6: Vision of a Ministry

It was at this time I paid a visit to the Evangelical Sisters of Mary at Canaan in Darmstadt, West Germany to learn more about the 'Joy-Filled Life' through repentance and pain. My time there showed me a new dimension of God's love, even though I only spent ten days with the Sisters and Canaan brothers. Their humility and total surrender to God's will in their lives is something I shall always remember and admire.

The time at Canaan, with the Sisters of Mary had not only helped to establish within me a 'first love' for Jesus, but also the need for much repentance. I thought I was pretty humble and aware of my inadequacies. Now I realised how judgemental I could be. Sometimes, in subtle ways, I had seen the 'speck' in my brother or sister's eye, when there was a great big plank in my own! Sins were uncovered that I had not realised were there. For example, the Lord showed me that I was conceited. 'How can I be,' I thought, 'when I am so shy and often aware of my weaknesses?' Mother Basilea pointed out that if we keep examining our actions in the mirror of our minds and continually wonder what others are thinking of us, then we are proud and conceited. It is a form of self-idolatry – that was me all right!

However, having returned from this heavy 'spiritual

injection' in my life, my lifestyle soon slipped into a fairly mundane pattern again. Working at the Church Hall and studying for my 'O' levels had filled nearly all my time. My father travelled over on my day off and spent nearly all the day with me. My relationships with most people were fairly superficial, compared to what I had experienced with Tim and John. They were still a part of my life, but not a lot was happening between us. We were certainly not as involved with one another as we had been. In the neighbourhood and church I had become very much a part of the environment. I was no longer the new Christian, whom the Lord had dramatically changed. I was now part of the 'establishment' at home, virtually all my social contact being with other Christians. My homosexual friends kept in touch, usually through Christmas cards. We always said it would be nice to meet up again, but without verbalising it, probably agreed that we no longer had much in common.

It was time to take stock. What had the Lord done in my life? Where do I go from here? It seemed probable that I would go forward again for ordination, eventually. I was still operating as a lay minister in the church, but usually needed a hefty kick before I would actually go out visiting. On every occasion I actually pushed myself out and started 'door knocking', the Lord blessed and uplifted me, considerably. Again and again I have seen how easy it is for Satan to convince me that I have nothing to give. Apathy sets in and a type of spiritual depression. Once that is broken through, the lies of the enemy are exposed, the Lord moves and blessings are received.

In July 1976 Gerald Coates wrote a very honest and well-balanced article about homosexuality in *Crusade Magazine* which meant a lot to me, because here was a Christian who had been prepared to share something of his homosexual past. I had still not talked with another Christian from a homosexual background. I felt I must write to *Crusade* and thank them, sharing a bit of my own experience, and wondered if I should use my address. Considering what I had shared in the letter, it seemed very hypocritical not to do so, but I felt rather exposed. As usual, I hesitated before taking any action. When the letter was finally sent it was too late for the edition carrying readers' reactions to Gerald's article. However, I noticed to my great relief that under every letter printed were the words, 'Name and address supplied'. 'Praise the Lord!' I thought, 'They won't print my name and address, after all!' A month later I received the next copy of *Crusade* from our church distributor, as I was leaving the Sunday morning service. I was outside the church with a couple of friends who knew me quite well and about a hundred other churchgoers. I opened my *Crusade* and rapidly turned to the 'Letters' section. My eyes suddenly spotted the words, 'Martin Hallett, Upton, Merseyside'. I screamed in horror. My friends turned towards me and I showed them the page. They laughed and said, 'Now you really have nailed your colours to the mast! Praise the Lord!' My stomach was still turning over, with embarrassment. It was a strange feeling, almost like being in a public place and suddenly realising that I had no clothes on (which happens to be a recurring nightmare of mine!)

I felt terribly self-conscious for several weeks. It made me realise that after my initial desire to be open with everyone when I first became a Christian, there were many people I knew in church who had had no idea of my background. One such person, a missionary home on furlough, came up to me after church one Sunday. She gently squeezed my arm and whispered in my ear, 'I saw your letter in *Crusade*. Praise the Lord – it's wonderful.'

There were one or two other quiet words of encouragement, which helped me to overcome my fears.

The repercussions from that letter were remarkable. Roy Barker had a phonecall from someone called Geoffrey Percival saying that he believed the person who wrote a letter in *Crusade* went to Roy's church. Geoffrey would be very interested to meet Martin Hallett because of a ministry that he and one or two people from the Nationwide Festival of Light were about to launch.

Eddy and Irene Stride, (Rector of Christchurch Spitalfields, London and his wife) have a wonderful gift of hospitality. Geoffrey Percival and Bob Hill were staying together at the Strides, where the topic of my letter in *Crusade* was mentioned. Geoff was on his way to Poole in Dorset to launch a new ministry to homosexuals, to be called Pilot. Bob had been a member of my church, St Mary's in the past and still had many friends there, and he certainly knew of me. Except for this 'God-incidence' of a meeting it is unlikely that I would have met Geoff. I could have found out about Pilot in the course of time, but may not have contacted him, except possibly for help – if my pride allowed it!

Some friends of mine in Upton offered me a holiday in Bournemouth, staying in their mother's house. This seemed an ideal opportunity to meet Geoff, whom I immediately got on well with. He was easy to relax with and reminded me a bit of my slightly eccentric friend, Richard, although Geoff had no 'upper class accent' and certainly not Richard's homosexual inclinations! Many years of experience with Eric Hutching's evangelistic team had left Geoff with much to share and give, and with the ability to communicate personal application of basic biblical principles clearly and often amusingly.

I was intrigued by the way he had converted the church

vestry from which he operated, into a 'home from home'. There was a nice green Wilton carpet covering the floor, a couple of smart chairs, desk and filing cabinet; also some cooking facilities and a portable television in the corner. It seemed more like a smart study or living room, than a church vestry. It was Geoff's little world. When not answering the phone, writing or seeing people, he would perhaps help to tidy the church graveyard outside or walk down to the harbour and town of Poole itself.

As Geoff and I talked, I became aware for the first time that there were some people professing to be born-again Christians, who believed that a homosexual relationship was compatible with Christianity. It really shocked me to read a letter written to Geoff by one of these people. It was not abusive in any way and talked about a personal relationship with Christ, in fact using all the evangelical language that I had come to identify with committed Christians who love the Lord Jesus. 'How could this person possibly believe God was pleased with and blessed his homosexual partnership?' I thought. It seemed to be so clear from the Scriptures that it was wrong. I had read books by David Field[1] and Roger Moss[2], which had served to underline my own thoughts on the subject. The early conviction that homosexual behaviour, but not orientation or temptation, was wrong had never been challenged. I had not really thought it through for myself yet. It just seemed that the texts by Paul and the attitude of Jesus in themselves were enough for me and now that I was firmly established in a Christian lifestyle which upheld my beliefs, I really did not want to change my point of view. So the beliefs of the person who wrote the

---

[1] *The Homosexual Way – A Christian Option* (IVP).
[2] *Christians and Homosexuality* (Paternoster).

letter left me puzzled, angry but at the same time challenged. It was reassuring to know that Geoff agreed with me.

I remembered my early Christian experience and realised how important the acceptance and understanding of other Christians had been to me. Certainly my relationships with Tim and John had brought a lot of love and fulfilment to my life. 'Was this not what all homosexuals are really searching for?' I thought. One evening, Geoff had an appointment to counsel a Christian man about his homosexual problems. He asked me if I would like to join them, and I agreed. I found myself becoming more and more fascinated by the prospect of actually meeting another Christian with homosexual feelings. It had always seemed as if there was just Tim and I who felt like this, although of course I knew there must be others. What would this man be like? Would he be attractive to me?

I was shocked at my reactions. There were hints of responses that I knew from my past. Was it more than just an old reflex action, or something much more serious? Whatever it was I knew it must be 'crucified with Christ'. The curiosity itself still lingered, until I actually met this man, but I knew there was no question of any relationship, sexual or not. I stopped analysing my feelings so much and decided that I would enter this situation, no matter what my motives and responses might be. When I eventually joined Geoff and his contact, all I could think of was helping and ministering to him.

My brief time with Geoffrey Percival in Poole had not only made me aware of the need for this type of ministry, but it gave me a burning desire to help in some way. As I mulled everything over in my mind and thought of my own experiences, some basic needs emerged that I felt were very important. It seemed to me that it was no good simply counselling people if there was not a church fellowship in which they would be loved, accepted and could grow in Christ. With all my complaints about being lonely, I remembered very clearly how unjudgmental and accepting Christians had been and still were to me. From what Geoff had shared about the fears and reluctance of many churches and individual Christians to face up to the homosexual issue, there seemed a very urgent need for positive teaching. If this did not happen, how many other Christians would join the ranks of the homosexual Christian who wrote to Geoff? Therefore, I thought the ideal type of ministry would be twofold; partly teaching the Church and partly counselling. I put these ideas down on paper, rather like a job description. I realised that I had created an idea for a workable ministry and wanted to give it some sort of title. The event of three years previously, when I released the trapped butterfly came into mind. Since that time I had seen so many ways in which the 'truth had set me free'.

Truth in terms of God's love.

Truth about myself in weakness and strength.

Truth in terms of honesty and openness with others. No more need to deceive or be a hypocrite.

All these and more had set me free in lots of ways, even though of course there was still a long way to go. Therefore the name must encompass somehow truth and freedom. I decided to call my idea 'True Freedom' and realised that God had given me this vision. When I thought of my little bit of counselling experience, the lay ministry and of course what I had been through in terms of my homosexuality, it seemed that the Lord had been preparing me for all this. Jesus said, 'Which of you, if his son asks for bread, will give him a stone?' (Matt. 7.9). The 'stone' that I thought had been my lot, when turned down for the ordained ministry, had really been 'bread'. It had been pointing that way to another door, which was just beginning to open.

Geoff shared with me the way the Lord led them to Pilot. It had originally been planned to open a care centre, sponsored by the Nationwide Festival of Light and run by Geoff and a retired Salvation Army worker, Edward Shackleton. The people living at the centre would be homosexuals and other casualties of the permissive society. A lack of sufficient funds seemed to indicate that another direction and ministry was needed and Pilot was born. Advertisements were placed in newspapers and a phone number given. Therefore, the majority of people contacting Pilot were not Christians. Mr Shackleton had a life long burden for this type of ministry and I hope and pray was encouraged by all God has done, when he went to be with the Lord, several years later in 1985.

I shared my vision of True Freedom with the Care Committee of the Nationwide Festival of Light. It was different in many ways to Pilot and they were keen to use it in conjunction with their own ministry. They were very helpful and a great encouragement to me, we had several meetings together and people like Raymond Johnston (now also with the Lord) as Director of NFOL (Nationwide Festival of Light) introduced me to other well known Christians interested in this subject. He also brought me into a Christian radio programme (called 'Sunday Supplement'), which was all very daunting for a shy person like me, but I was learning to depend more on the Lord to give me confidence.

Gordon Landreth (then General Secretary of Evangelical Alliance) also heard about me and I was invited to take part in some discussions they were organising. These were between three evangelical Christians who supported homosexual relationships in certain situations and three who did not. I was introduced to the discussions after the initial meeting. This meant there were four contributors with personal experience of homosexuality, but I was the only one who believed that all homosexual sex was wrong. The atmosphere was good on the whole and I was impressed by the graciousness of all involved.

It was on this programme that I met Jean White, the Pastor of the London Metropolitan Community Church. She struck me as a warm, friendly and very 'homely' person, from a Brethren background, who believed that the Bible, and therefore God, approved of some homosexual relationships where love and commitment were involved. Tom Jones, another member of the group talked about his own Methodist background and involvement in a long-term homosexual relationship. Tom also impressed me, but I could not agree with his viewpoint. Those of us who disagreed with Tom and Jean were surprised to admit, as we prayed together, that we had experienced Christian fellowship. I know this would be difficult for many to accept, and it certainly was a surprise for me, until I realised that we are all guilty of compromising God's truth in some part of our lives, because we are all sinners. Obviously, we must seek to put any disobedient or sinful area right with God. But the fact still remains that there will be sins still not, as yet, revealed to us. I do believe that people involved in homosexual relationships, no matter how stable or loving they may be, are disobeying God (more of this in a later chapter) but I can understand how they have come to that point of view. Both Jean and Tom had been badly hurt by misunderstanding Christians. They had struggled against their homosexual feelings. Then a relationship had developed which met so many of their needs for love and affirmation.

Genital sexual expression seems a 'natural' expression of their love for one another. People in this position feel such a measure of personal fulfilment that it is confused with the peace God brings to our lives. They therefore assume that the relationship is blessed by God and seek to find biblical approval for this. I think anyone honestly seeking to understand biblical truth and accepting the Bible's authority, cannot question its condemnation of active homosexual relationships. However, it is very easy to compromise when emotional and sexual feelings are so strong. Just as many from an evangelical background have, like Tom and Jean, joined the so-called 'gay church', there are also those who come out of churches like MCC because they come under strong conviction from the Holy Spirit that their views on homosexual relationships are wrong.

These meetings were certainly an 'eye-opener' for me. They also introduced me to the Rev David Field, from Oak Hill College, whose book *The Homosexual Way – A Christian Option?* had helped me a lot at that time. David and his wife Margaret have since been a tremendous source of encouragement to me. Their God-given love, gentleness and humility are wonderful.

The meetings with the Care Committee of NFOL continued, but despite all the good intentions it did not seem to be possible to employ me along with Geoff. However, Roy Barker had been very much aware of all that was happening and was convinced that this area of ministry was right for me.

One Wednesday evening, when I was preparing to lock up the Church Hall, Roy asked how the talks with NFOL were going. He thought for a moment and said, 'I don't see why we can't start a ministry up here in the north. Let's see . . . we could set up a trust. Who would we need? A solicitor – yes, I can think of someone. A headmaster . . . yes. A treasurer . . . . Martin you contact Raymond and say that if they are not able to take you on, we can start something here. See what he says.'

I contacted Raymond who thought it was a great idea. 'Right!' Roy said when I told him. 'Come to the vicarage next Tuesday morning and we'll talk some more about this.'

I arrived at Roy's study, expecting a fairly brief talk with him about my future and the idea of a trust. His life was so full of meetings and appointments, in no way did I expect that he would be able to spend much time with me at such short notice. How wrong I was. Miraculously, Roy always seemed to have the time whenever there was an urgent need for his ministry. We spent all morning and afternoon together, Barbara (Roy's wife) re-fuelling us with coffee and a snack for lunch. In that time, Roy had phoned all the people he saw as potential trustees and used his normal methods of persuasiveness. They all agreed and a meeting was arranged. Then the Council of Reference was contacted and agreed to have their names associated with the work. A plan of action was made by Roy. A phone, office, leaflet, adverts, typewriter, filing cabinet and so on were provided and organised. I was given a list of tasks that I could do, including the wording for the leaflet. Roy felt that the True Freedom Trust should be something of an umbrella title, in case in the future other areas of ministry were brought in. He thought the teaching and counselling parts should be given separate names, to give us flexibility. Because of our very close links with Pilot and the vision for many Pilots around the country which had been discussed by the Care Committee, I assumed we could use the name 'Pilot' for the counselling ministry. We spent ages trying to think of a name that would link with Pilot for the teaching ministry.

Originally, the reason for the name had been a nautical one – a ship in distress being led to safety by the pilot. The only linking word we could think of was 'chandler' (refurbishing and equipping the ship). So it was decided – the ministries would be called Pilot and Chandler.

Roy wasted no time. When a letter appeared about homosexuality in the *Church Times* he responded, mentioning that two ministries existed, called Pilot and Chandler. This was even before the leaflet had been printed! It was just as well, because NFOL spotted the letter and graciously, but understandably pointed out that if we were going to use the name Pilot then they should be involved in the trust and ministry, to some extent. They were quite right, of course. Roy and I did not feel this would be practical and would make the ministry very cumbersome. We wanted it to be northern based, for convenience, even though it would serve the whole country. We would therefore have to think of another name, which was very difficult (since that time, I have come across many good names of similar ministries and wished I had thought of them first!) Despite much thought and prayer, inspiration just did not come our way. Eventually, a music group at church whose name had been Harbinger, meaning 'messenger' split up. I liked the name and they agreed to let me use it. Some time afterwards I was amused to see one or two ex-members of the group wearing a T-shirt with 'Harbinger' emblazoned on the front. My wicked sense of humour put thoughts in my mind of what people who knew about us might think if they saw them wearing these shirts! We wanted to retain the word 'Chandler' because Roy had already publicised it, if only in the *Church Times*.

It was decided that I would work from home and continue with my job at the Church Hall, until we had enough funds to pay my salary and the Lord had supplied my replacement for the job at church. We spent a long time preparing the leaflet and a booklet called *Homosexuality – An Explanation*. All our material would be printed on the church's litho machine. I would prepare the material and give it to Roy, who then chopped, changed and condensed it. Eventually it was all set up and printed. Advertisements were put in many Christian papers and a letter sent to all local evangelical churches on Merseyside, seeking support. The Trust Deed was signed on 29th June 1977. Once again, a great debt of gratitude was due to Roy for all his loving concern and wisdom. True Freedom Trust was now in operation and we awaited the response.

7: Growth of a Ministry

Initially, we thought of having an office in Liverpool. One of our trustees owned a Christian Centre and there was a possibility of using one of the rooms. Eventually it was decided to sell the building, so that venture did not materialise. However, we had already applied for a Post Office Box in the area and used this address in our adverts and literature. The Post Office Box given us was No. 8 and the postal district Liverpool 8. I hope it was not superstition, but I did wonder if the numbers chosen were a nice little humorous touch from the Lord!

The people from the Centre kindly collected the mail for me. However, travelling over to Liverpool from Upton was rather expensive, because of a tunnel under the River Mersey, which has a toll fee. So, after a few months we decided to move the PO Box to Upton and use the phone number of my home, given out discreetly.

The initial adverts had been in the *Church Times, Crusade, Life of Faith, The Church of England Newspaper* and *Methodist Recorder*. We were obviously carefully vetted before being accepted by these publications for inclusion in the personal column. The advertisements read:

HOMOSEXUALITY – Biblically-based counselling (Harbinger)/teaching (Chandler) ministries. Free booklet – foolscap sae: True Freedom Trust, PO Box 8, Liverpool L8 1YL.

Initially, many of the people responding to our adverts represented homosexual organisations seeking to find out where we stood. Occasionally there would be one or two strong comments, denouncing us and all we believed. Some clergy argued against us, especially on our stand for scriptural authority. Then there were many more people who wrote expressing appreciation that at last some Christians were taking a stand against homosexuality, but in a positive way. I was not inundated with mail at that time, it was more of a steady trickle. I kept thinking that the Lord must have a strange sense of humour, giving me a ministry which consisted mainly of writing letters to people. This had always been quite an ordeal. I was so self-conscious about my layout and grammar, wondering what people might think of me. The most difficult letters of course were the replies to people with homosexual problems. They were nearly all Christians. Some had never shared their difficulties with anyone else before. I realised very early on that I would have to devise a simple form of coding that would preserve anonymity, just in case anyone broke into my house and tried blackmail. It was very unlikely that anyone would know where I lived, but I wanted to be able to assure people who contacted us of very strict confidentiality, which is vital in this kind of ministry, as in any other. This need had been highlighted for me when I worked for the Samaritans: their own filing system and confidentiality had impressed me tremendously.

I therefore devised a system of coding which meant that none of the letters sent or other confidences given by people could be linked with them. Only people directly involved in the ministry of TFT would know who had contacted us for help. I just had to make sure that I could understand my own coding system!

I found it very difficult to answer the pleas for help

from Christians struggling with homosexuality. I was only too aware from past experience how easily I could be misunderstood or sound very trite and unsympathetic. Quite a lot of prayer was also needed as I struggled with my grammar for each letter, sitting at the old oak desk in my bedroom, gazing from the window into my garden below and the backs of the modern semis beyond. I had bought a Burmese cat by this time, who was completely dependent on me, following everywhere I went and jumping on my lap at the slightest opportunity. Misty is small, slim and grey with specks of cream. She also talks a lot and at this early time of her life she often made a lot of noise! In a way it was a comfort to me, as I sat with a letter in front of me, poised at the typewriter with Misty on my lap. Sometimes it seemed that her gentle murmurings were joining me in prayer for inspiration. I decided that it was best to express some of my fears and anxieties to the recipient of the letter, in a way to prepare him or her for any misinterpretation. I still do this and ask the person to respond with any questions, comments or criticisms. I found in this way it was possible to strike up quite a relationship with someone through a letter. Even when I gave my phone number, very few people were prepared to use it. Letters, somehow seemed safer. None of my correspondents lived locally.

Eventually, someone did decide to come and see me, all the way from London. At first it was only going to be for a day visit, but I gave him the option of staying overnight, if he wished. So many feelings went through my mind as I waited for him to arrive at the railway station. Imagine coming all the way from London to see me! What was he expecting? Would he be disappointed?

The arrangements for meeting amused me a little, but there was also a sense in which they reminded me of my 'degenerate days' and I wondered if it was right to think it funny.

'How will I know you?'

'I will be wearing a blue anorak. I'm tall, dark and . . . bald!'

Once we had met only the fears of his expectations remained. He already knew something of my testimony, so I decided that I must initially listen carefully to what he was and was not saying. Occasionally I would encourage him to talk by making it clear that I understood most of what happens in the homosexual scene. I therefore would not be shocked by any of his revelations. My ideology of the homosexual's basic search for love was being confirmed. A man desperately searching for love and longing to be able to find it in the heterosexual Christian world, but somehow unable to do so. No matter how many times he tried to grit his teeth and overcome his homosexual feelings, he would slip into homosexual bars and other meeting places, not necessarily making any social contact, but feeling accepted and loved when surrounded by others with homosexual feelings. In keeping with many others who were to visit me, this man said that I was the first Christian he had met who experienced homosexual feelings and yet was not involved in a homosexual lifestyle. Eventually he decided that he would stay overnight and travel back the next morning. As we talked I found various needs in his life highlighted and I could see how God could well want them to be met, but it was not easy. It would mean making himself very vulnerable to other Christians and what would happen if they did not respond? How could I possibly guarantee that they would understand? Most people contacting us, having not shared their difficulties with other Christians, are fairly convinced they will be misunderstood and rejected. Such rejection may not be in terms of a positive decision or verbalised statement. It is more likely to be a much more subtle rejection, often not recognised as such by the person guilty of it. I still find myself at fault in this area myself in regard to my attitude to my homosexual friends, even today. Because I find I cannot identify with them and sometimes even feel uncomfortable in their company for many different reasons, I avoid the situation and make few steps towards them. I may not want to admit that I have rejected them, but in fact I have done just that.

Some Christians, because of their lack of real understanding of the homosexual person, plus a misinterpretation of the biblical references, make a much more positive decision to reject. They decide that they will not even 'eat with such a person'. The reasoning behind this stems from some words of the Apostle Paul to Christians at Corinth, 'But now I am writing you that you must not associate with anyone who calls himself a brother but is sexually immoral or greedy, an idolater or a slanderer, a drunkard or a swindler. With such a man do not even eat' (1 Cor. 5.11). These are difficult verses, but they are not referring to someone seeking to overcome a particular sin, but rather a Christian who actually accepts sinful behaviour and perhaps 'they not only continue to do these very things but also approve of those who practise them' (Rom. 1. 32b). With such a person a Christian is not to have intimate fellowship partly, I feel sure, to encourage the person to see what is wrong. Paul is therefore not referring to someone struggling with homosexual feelings and temptations.

There is also a failure amongst Christians to recognise that homosexual feelings or orientation are not a personal choice, although putting them into practice, of course, is. Most importantly, it must be realised that the sexually immoral person is not mentioned in isolation. An idolater, slanderer, drunkard, swindler or greedy person is also to be treated in the same way. Can any of us really say we have never been guilty of any of these sins? I am sure many of us have been guilty and unrepentant, at times.

Many Christians have been greatly hurt by this type of unbiblical judgmentalism. I began to find that some of the people who contacted me had believed that even a homosexual orientation is wrong in God's eyes. It was a wonderful experience to know of the joy and relief felt by them, when I opened up God's Word and we saw that it is only homosexual sexual acts that are condemned in Scripture. I was amazed by the number of Christians with homosexual feelings who had never knowingly met another homosexual, let alone been involved in sexual activity.

Some of the people contacting me live a kind of double existence; on the one hand being very involved with Christian fellowship, but then slipping into homosexual activity compulsively – usually the anonymous type of one-off sexual encounters, experiencing a sudden giving in to temptation, followed, of course, by tremendous guilt. Then pornography, seems to be an enormous problem for many Christians, often people without experience of homosexual relationships at all. Pornography soon becomes an addiction, once sexual pleasure has been gained from it. Almost every magazine stand is a fascination and causes real temptation. Homosexual pornography is not as readily available as its heterosexual counterpart, but in some ways that can make the search for it a compulsive, soul destroying drive. Again and again the same story would be told, 'I pick up the pornography, use it perhaps once or twice, feel disgusted with myself and destroy it. Then I find myself in the shop again . . . '

In my early days as a Christian I would have thought, if not said, 'The answer to these sorts of problems is easy – claim the Lord's victory and fight the temptation in the strength of that victory.' Praise the Lord, that for many it really is just as straightforward as that. I was now able to be thankful that God allowed me to experience difficulties and problems of one sort and another (and still does) because this enabled me to identify with so many of the desperately hurting people who were contacting me. I felt I could share something of Paul's experience, 'Praise be to the God and Father of our Lord Jesus Christ, the Father of compassion and the God of all comfort, who comforts us in all our troubles so that we can comfort those in any trouble with the comfort we ourselves have received from God. For just as the sufferings of Christ flow over into our lives, so also through Christ our comfort overflows. If we are distressed, it is for your comfort and salvation; if we are comforted it is for your comfort, which produces in you patient endurance of the same sufferings we suffer' (2 Cor. 1.3–7). I always find these verses tremendously encouraging. They help to give a positive reason for present and past problems, trials and difficulties of all sorts. My past experiences were beginning to have some purpose for my present ministry. God was using me, not despite all I have been and am today, but because of it. I was able to share this with others seeking my help. I hope not as a glib answer to their problems, but at least as some measure of encouragement. Many of these hurting people had such a low self-image. They felt 'dirty' and 'abnormal', longing to have heterosexual feelings, 'like everyone else'. My experiences in Upton, especially with one or two women I knew, encouraged me to ask if it was appreciated that heterosexual people often have sexual problems too. Inevitably, the reply would be, 'Do they really? I suppose they must have . . . I wish I had heterosexual problems, at least they're normal.'

I had been blessed in many ways through my relationships with Tim and John. I soon realised that for many of the Christians I was meeting in 'TFT', this was out of the question. They were fearful of becoming sexually attracted to anyone of the same sex they grew close to. They were fearful of sharing their problems with others, in case they were rejected. They were fearful of a lonely old age. Sometimes they even feared their salvation had been lost.

Scripture tells us, 'There is no fear in love. But perfect love drives out fear, because fear has to do with punishment. The man who fears is not made perfect in love' (1 John 4.18). How I longed to help these men and women grow more towards being 'made perfect in love'. How I longed to experience more of that in my own life! In these early days, I was beginning to see beneath the 'presenting problems' to the underlying needs that God wanted to meet. In many situations I felt able to suggest ways in which God could meet these needs – but it was always within the context of the Body of Christ (The Church). Nearly every time I had the frustration of seeing how God could bring fulfilment and joy to the person's life, but knowing full well that it would be unlikely that their church would meet the necessary needs. While this was primarily a failing in the fellowship, the person concerned would often be unprepared to take the risk of finding the necessary love within the Body of Christ. If you are convinced you are not lovable and will therefore not be loved by others, you tend to wait for them to make the first move towards you. This is certainly my experience. But it is a vicious circle, because others then feel you do not want them, your low self-image having made you withdraw behind a mask. You therefore drive away the very love for which you long.

At this stage of my ministry I did not delve much into the reasons for the lack of self-love. The priority seemed more and more to help the churches become better places for hurting people to know the healing power of God's love being expressed through his people. This means much more teaching about sensitive subjects like homosexuality, so that people with problems would know they were understood, loved and accepted. It also means more teaching about loving one another in Christ.

I found that I was seeking to provide something of the love and encouragement that should have been coming from the Church. It was a tremendous privilege to share in the deepest secrets of a person's life. To hear someone say, 'I have never told this to anyone else before,' is a truly moving experience. Many felt a tremendous burden lifted by simply sharing, for the first time in a completely honest way, with someone they felt understood them. I was staggered to know just how far people would travel, just to be able to do this. It was quite common for someone to come from the other end of the country. In many cases they would even be unable to stay overnight and travelled back the same day. It was always daunting – I feared they were expecting too much. Sometimes I almost wished I could pay their train fare so that they would not be too disappointed. Thankfully, no one actually felt they had wasted their money, although the Lord had not always ministered in the way they expected. So often it was imagined that one visit to me would suddenly turn them into heterosexuals!

The people I found most difficult to deal with were those who had become disillusioned with evangelical Christians. Often they had been prayed with, anointed and 'delivered' – but with still no release from the homosexual feelings. There was sometimes a temporary absence of sexual thoughts when experiencing the power of the Holy Spirit, but it was not sustained. I did not find this difficult to understand. After all, if one is suddenly overwhelmed by the love and power of God, sexual thoughts are unlikely to be at the forefront of the mind. Sometimes, it seems especially for women, the experience of being filled with the Holy Spirit takes the lid off deeply buried emotions. The result can actually be an awareness of homosexual feelings, perhaps for the first time in the person's life.

As more people began contacting us for help and church leaders were seeking more information and advice, the financial support of the ministry increased. Only a couple of people were covenanting or giving on a regular basis, but the commitment was growing. We hoped it would not be too long before I was able to relinquish my job at the Church Hall and work for TFT full-time. I was obviously restricted in terms of time spent outside the parish. One or two speaking engagements were beginning to appear. This vital part of our ministry was the most daunting for me. I remember going to Southampton University, having been invited by Eddy Stride's son, Stephen. He was a good looking young man with a mass of fair, curly hair and a warm, friendly effervescent character. It was so exhilarating to be with him. His enthusiasm to share the gospel was balanced with a warmth and desire to understand. He did not seem threatened in any way or nervous when in the company of a homosexual at the college, who quite blatantly made several verbal 'passes' at him, in terms of comments about his good looks.

Despite all this I was tremendously nervous and phoned John to ask him to pray for me. It seemed quite likely that there would be at least some opposition. The meeting hall was very large and smartly designed, with seating in the form of broad carpeted steps. As Stephen and I watched the students arriving, he would say, 'Oh he's from the Gay Soc [Gay Society, a university club] – a really militant guy. He's a Marxist . . . ' and so on. I tried to retain some composure. I decided that one of the main reasons for my nerves was the fear of looking stupid – making a fool of myself.

This was really pride (remembering my Canaan experience). I tried to give it to the Lord and allow myself to feel secure in him. All I can say is that the Holy Spirit really did take control and once the meeting was under way, I was amazed at myself. I felt I should start by sharing something of my apprehensions and fears, knowing how I expected the gay militants to respond. I was amazed at their reaction. There was more respect, even if they disagreed, than I anticipated. Oh that more Christians could have Stephen's zeal and enthusiasm!

Needless to say, the response from churches was very poor indeed. Less than a handful of local churches responded to the letter Roy Barker had distributed.

There was now to be a change in the situation at home, which greatly affected the course of our ministry. Since my mother's death, father lived on his own in Liverpool and obviously felt lonely. He used to come over once a week on my day off, or I would travel over to Liverpool. He raised the idea of us moving in together, which I resisted at first, but then thought it could work if we had two living rooms so that I could entertain my friends without it interfering with him. We eventually found a pre-war detached house in Upton, which had remained empty for many years and had not been decorated since 1949! It needed a lot of money spending on it, but had great potential. The large rear garden had woodland at the end and was not overlooked. Although it only had three bedrooms, it seemed to be full of small rooms – larders, cloak rooms, wash rooms and storage rooms. We managed to persuade the owner to sell it and set to work with renovations. The Lord's hand could clearly be seen in the whole situation, partly because of the ease with which we had sold our own modern houses. My only regret, later, was that we had not done more internal structural alterations, knocking some of the rooms together and making a better kitchen. We managed with a very small, fairly old fashioned kitchen and a morning-room. I know my mother would not have approved, but I think in some ways the smaller old fashioned rooms, morning-room and larder reminded father of bygone days. It was not easy at first readjusting to living with one's parent, after so many years 'out of the nest'. I also found myself reluctant to share many things with father, possibly because this had become a 'natural' reaction when I was involved in a homosexual lifestyle. Father adapted wonderfully, however, and it was a great joy to see him moving on spiritually. I am sure this work of the Holy Spirit in his life started primarily after my mother died, although there had always been a 'simple faith' there since his childhood days as a choirboy in the West Country town of Shepton Mallet.

Meanwhile, at church we had built a large extension, because the original Victorian building was too small for the congregation. There had also been a refurbishing of the Church Halls, through a job-creation scheme. One of the leaders of this, a qualified joiner, was offered the job of full-time maintenance man and Hallkeeper. This was an answer to prayer and a fulfilment of Roy's vision. My caretaking at the Church Hall had only been thought of as a temporary measure, even though it lasted for nearly four years. It was now obviously the right time to take the step of faith and work for TFT full-time. In February 1978, I became the self-employed staff worker of TFT, being paid fifteen pounds per week by the Trust, plus a five pound retainer by the church, for some part-time verging duties.

My father's standard of living, as far as food goes, was completely different to my own and I could not afford to keep up with it. He very generously agreed to subsidise me in this way as part of his support for the ministry. He found his own ministry in feeding me and the guests who came to stay, usually for counselling.

At first I found it very difficult to adjust to the new work routine. I felt guilty if I was not actually doing something for TFT. I had been conditioned that working for wages involved manual activity. Reading, thinking and even praying, did not seem like work. I guess this must be a common problem for people coming into full-time Christian work from a manual occupation. We had the phone transferred from my other house and used exclusively as a TFT phone, in my little office at home. There was just enough room for a desk and a chair, which faced the window, looking out on the long garden. My only storage space consisted of an old kitchen cupboard, which just fitted on the back wall, and two wide shelves on the other walls. The rough brickwork and simple hardboard lined roof meant there were regular showers of brick dust! However, my determination to have my own office (there was no room for anyone else, anyway) rather than working from a bedroom made it all seem worthwhile, at first.

Roy was always keen on 'door knocking'. It was one of the reasons his ministry in Upton had been so blessed by the Lord. Now he was convinced that this was also essential for TFT. The difference being that I would not be knocking on the doors of householders, but vicars and pastors. Visiting as a lay minister had given me some experience in this field, but I always hated going out on my own. Now I had to face this and another problem as well. It did not take me long to realise that the pastors and vicars were often very suspicious, or at least uneasy, about my theological stand. I could feel them scrutinising me mentally, as I shared what I believed God said about homosexuality and the basis and vision of the ministry. After a while there would be a release of this tension and I was often made to feel very much at home. Sometimes I was even invited in for a meal. However, every time I approached the idea of raising the subject in the church, there were tremendous reservations. 'I don't think the elders would approve. It's too delicate a subject.'

'I don't think we have anyone with this problem in our church, but we will know where to come if we do come across anybody. Could we contact you?'

I would try to point out that not only may some of their congregation have homosexual feelings, but the much wider implications raised by this subject are relevant and important for all Christians. This did not seem to impress them. Several attempts at door-knocking on local evangelical leaders' doors failed to produce even one speaking engagement. I plucked up courage and phoned a few local church leaders who were not known to be evangelicals. I had some varied responses:

'I am not sure that we have what you would term a fellowship, but I am interested in your point of view.'

'I am absolutely amazed that anyone can believe what you believe. I would happily bless a couple of men or women, if they asked me. I've never met anyone who believes in the Genesis story!'

However, despite all this negative response, speaking engagements were beginning to happen: I was given invitations by a couple of theological colleges; Oak Hill College, London and Trinity College, Bristol. At first this was tremendously daunting for a non-academic like me. When students and staff would chat beforehand and mention 'my lecture', I frequently felt like saying, 'I don't lecture really, you know, I'm not clever enough. I just talk and share.'

After the session, much to my amazement, students and even some of the lecturers, showed a lot of interest and treated me with much respect and admiration. I was just beginning to realise that Christian academics, whom I used to find very threatening, were vulnerable human beings themselves. This point was driven home to me even more forcibly when they started to come for personal help and advice.

A few invitations came from universities and colleges, mainly through the Christian Unions, which was encouraging. I was certainly gaining a little more self confidence, but on every occasion I had to surrender to Christ my fears of looking stupid and desires to impress.

I especially remember two meetings where there was some opposition. The first was at Liverpool University and had been organised by John. I opened up by saying that if anyone had told me six years ago I would be addressing a Christian meeting on this subject, I would have thought they were crazy. I shared my shyness and homosexual background. There were a couple of people in the audience who had known me slightly in my days on the 'gay scene'. One commented afterwards, 'I have listened to everything you said this evening and the only thing I agree with is what you said at the very beginning about never believing this would be possible for you.' The other meeting had been organised by the Festival of Light and was held in a meeting room over the shops in Regent Street, London. The room was packed with people and David Field was the speaker. I joined him on the platform, with Eddy Stride and Edward Shackleton. It was an intimate atmosphere inasmuch as the audience were tightly packed and very close to the platform.

As I glanced towards them, waiting for David to speak, it was very obvious that many of them were likely to be fairly militant. The atmosphere that made me believe this is difficult to describe. In some ways they seemed already angry and impatient, perhaps even like defiant children, determined to shock and offend. I could feel the tension and nerves in the pit of my stomach. What was I going to be expected to do and say?

David started speaking and immediately there were heckles and comments. It was very difficult, if not impossible to hear what David was saying. Because of the relatively small size of the room, there was no amplification. It became even noisier and a group of people near the front started to tear out pages from a large family Bible and throw them at the stage. Eddy Stride kept telling David to continue speaking from his notes, because the talk was being recorded. I guess it was thought that David was close enough to the recorder's microphone to prevent any other noises drowning him on the tape, but it seemed a bizarre situation. Some wondered if the meeting should be stopped, but that would be admitting defeat. If the people causing the disturbance refused to leave or be quiet it would again be playing into their hands to either force them out or call the police. There had already been an ugly incident in All Soul's Church, involving some gay Christians, which attracted bad publicity. The audience (mainly the militants that is) demanded a time for questions. A few people pointed at me and said, in a rather mocking tone, 'We want to know what you do to gay people on Merseyside?' It reminded me of the 'cages' from my brief boarding school days. I tried to be as positive and sensitive as possible. I explained where most of the people in touch with us stood and that many had contacted organisations agreeing with their point of view, rather than ours, but found they were unable to help. I can't remember much else of what I shared that evening, but I was aware, as never before, of a special anointing from the Lord. At one stage a woman called out, 'Why don't you send us all to the gas chambers? That's what you really want!' To my utter amazement I shouted back, 'If the day that happens ever arrives, then I will be first in the queue for the gas chamber!' Looking back, I am not sure if that was the wisest comment to make!

Afterwards a number of people from organisations who support some types of homosexual relationships within the Church, came up to David and saying they did not want to be associated with the more militant members of the audience.

I found that experiences like this one have left me with a sense of feeling threatened, when in the company of people involved in a homosexual lifestyle. I tend to assume they hate me, because they believe that Christians like myself strongly disapprove of them. The feelings of fear and anger that come across at meetings like this one have obviously not left me completely unscarred, emotionally. I never cease to admire those Christians who constantly have to suffer that sort of opposition because of their faith. I know the coward in me would make me want to run a mile, even though I know God always comes to our rescue.

8: Crisis of Faith – What Does the Bible Say?

The ministry was now quite well established and although many Christians and church fellowships were reluctant to support TFT as perhaps they would other societies, there were some very committed people behind us. Financially, there was not enough regular or covenanted giving to pay my salary, but the Lord provided for all our financial needs. We often wondered if we should take a further step of faith and spend money we did not have, expecting the Lord to provide it. In our situation this seemed wrong until there was very clear guidance from our heavenly Father. I was beginning to enjoy talking to Christian groups and was gaining some more confidence.

Then, early in 1979, I read a book, originating from America, by two Christian women from an evangelical background. Neither was apparently homosexual. They came down on the side of supporting homosexual relationships in certain situations. Many of their arguments were not new to me. They were basically echoing what the more 'liberal' theologians were saying, but it was dressed up in evangelical terminology. The two main points which impressed me were their arguments against the hurt and prejudice shown by many Christians and churches (having seen something of this) and the fact that they were not homosexual themselves and therefore unbiased.

Needless to say, reading this book left me very unsettled and insecure. I was not convinced that they were right, but still wondered if I could be wrong. Up to this point I had tended to accept much of what I was reading on the subject of homosexuality, because I agreed and could understand the strong biblical basis on which it was all founded. Perhaps I had not really thought it all out thoroughly for myself. I felt lonely and frightened, especially as I was due to make my second or third visit to Oak Hill College in two days. What on earth was I going to say? How could I speak with a strong sense of conviction? I dreaded the thought of it, but knew I must phone David Field and tell him how I was feeling. We would probably have to cancel the visit, but what about the future of TFT? How many people would I be letting down?

David was marvellous – he said that he understood and would like me to come and speak to his students anyway. 'Just share how you feel with them,' he said. David asked me to say more about my doubts and uncertainties. In his soft gentle voice he graciously shared that he knew the book in question. He felt himself that they were really echoing what John McNeil (the Roman Catholic author) had said. Apparently their translation of the Greek words in the relevant verses was not at all accurate (David was teaching New Testament Greek). What encouraged me most of all in David's attitude were his words, 'Martin, all I can say is that every time I read a new book published on this subject I pray that I may be convinced that my views are wrong. I have seen some of the agony experienced by Christians with homosexual feelings. However, this book did not convince me at all.' (Since that time, both David and I have seen something more of what God can do in terms of positive help and healing. It may be that he would add something a little more positive, today.)

Before going to Oak Hill I also went to see a Christian student friend in York, who had homosexual feelings. He was firm and positive with me. I could imagine myself telling someone else what he was saying to me! He was so loving and concerned that he phoned me at Tim's sister's house, where I was staying before I went to Oak Hill simply to say that he and one or two others were praying for me. His love and concern meant so much.

Over these few days I had been forced into doing a lot of thinking and praying. Eventually, just in time for my visit to Oak Hill I felt more positive and secure in my beliefs. This had been a painful, but necessary experience. It helped me to see how easily convinced someone with strong homosexual feelings could be by the arguments of a more liberal theology, when disguised by evangelicalism.

What does the Bible say about homosexual relationships? In Genesis 19.1–29 the famous story of Sodom and Gomorrah is used in all the various debates about homosexuality. Many have said that a society which tolerates and even encourages homosexuality is in danger of experiencing God's judgment in the same way. Lot was entertaining two angels then – 'Before they had gone to bed, all the men from every part of the city of Sodom – both young and old – surrounded the house. They called to Lot, "Where are the men who came to you tonight? Bring them out to us so that we can have sex with them" ' (Gen. 19.4, 5).

Some argue that the sin of Sodom in this context is a breach of hospitality. The word used ('yadha') can mean, 'to know' in terms of acquaintance. However, this seems very unlikely when Lot offered his virgin daughters to the men, so that the angels would not be abused – a tremendous willingness to sacrifice. As the NIV puts it, the men of Sodom wanted 'sex with them'. The scripture also says that 'all the men from every part of the city' were involved –

does this mean that they were all of a homosexual orientation? Many would say that is impossible, but in some cultures the ultimate form of insult is to rape a man. Sodom was a city in which just about every type of sexual perversion and immoral behaviour was rife. In that kind of environment they would not necessarily have needed a strong homosexual desire to motivate them – their action could simply be compared with mob violence or vandalism. I have never met any homosexual person who would agree with this type of homosexual behaviour. So is it relevant to the debate, as far as Christians are concerned? Not in terms of questioning whether a homosexual partnership is legitimate when love is involved.

We need to go on to look at what Ezekiel says about the sins of Sodom, in Ezekiel 16.49. 'Now this was the sin of your sister Sodom: She and her daughters were arrogant, overfed and unconcerned; they did not help the poor and needy. They were haughty and did detestable things before me. Therefore I did away with them as you have seen.' The homosexuality, of whatever type, was not the only sin of Sodom. There was a moral decadence and selfish disregard for those in need. Is that very different from our own western culture, today? Are we not also to be held accountable for much of the poverty and starvation in the Third World, because of our greed and unconcern?

Leviticus 18.22 says, 'Do not lie with a man as one lies with a woman; that is detestable' and in Leviticus 20.13 the death penalty is prescribed for such behaviour, as it is also for adultery and cursing one's father or mother. Many argue that Levitical prohibition is not applicable today, because laws also mentioned here include not wearing 'clothing woven of two kinds of material' not planting a 'field with two kinds of seed' and so on. However, I do not believe we can dismiss the reference to homosexuality that lightly. It seems to me that God was teaching his people not to 'do as they do in Egypt' or in the 'land of Canaan, where I am bringing you' (Lev. 18.3). Some of the laws are clearly related to a culture and lifestyle of that time, but others were also linked with much more basic aspects of human nature or behaviour, as were the ten commandments. Looking at the context of the homosexual prohibition (i.e. unlawful sexual relations) it would seem to be clearly building on the ten commandments in terms of rules for human behaviour.

It was reading the Gospels, rather than the usual 'proof texts' of the Old Testament which initially helped to convince me that homosexual relationships were wrong as far as God is concerned. The Gospels do not carry any explicit reference to homosexual relationships, but I believe we need to look at Jesus' words in Matthew 19.11, 12. Jesus had been talking with the disciples about marriage and divorce, a difficult and sensitive area. The disciples, with typical human reasoning replied, 'If this is the situation between a husband and wife, it is better not to marry.' Jesus says, 'Not everyone can accept this teaching, but only those to whom it has been given. For some are eunuchs because they were born that way; others were made that way by men; and others have renounced marriage [or made themselves eunuchs] because of the kingdom of heaven'. The Greek word 'eunouchos' does not necessarily mean someone castrated, but a person who is celibate or not involved in sexual activity. Jesus is therefore making a profound statement for members of God's Kingdom, which is a clarification of teaching which has appeared in the Old Testament. He is saying that 'you will either be married, or living without sexual relationships.' The three reasons that the Lord gives for someone being in this situation would include people with homosexual orientation.

It is also very important to realise that in biblical times there was no identity based on a sexual orientation, as we know it today; in fact I do not think it was imagined that anyone would be strictly limited to one type of sexual temptation. Sexuality and human sexual behaviour was seen in a much wider perspective, and people did not consider that homosexual behaviour would only be limited to a certain group of people with that type of orientation. The words 'homosexual' and 'heterosexual' have only been introduced within the last couple of hundred years.

The Apostle Paul mentions homosexual relationships much more explicitly. For example, in Romans 1 he is talking about mankind's disobedience to a holy God by rejecting the truth about him and the pattern of living the Lord has set for his creation. Some of the results of this disobedience are spelt out by Paul, 'Therefore God gave them over in the sinful desires of their hearts to sexual impurity for the degrading of their bodies with one another . . . ' (v. 24) and ' . . . God gave them over to shameful lusts. Even the women exchanged natural relations for unnatural ones. In the same way the men also abandoned natural relations with women and were inflamed with lust for one another. Men committed indecent acts with other men, and received in themselves the due penalty for their perversion.' The 'exchange' Paul talks about is the exchange of 'truth about God' (v. 25) and his plan for creation for worthless images or idols. The words used to describe 'natural' and 'unnatural' (physin and paraphysin) mean contrary to God's perfect nature, not contrary to human nature. There is a tremendous difference because, since the Fall, none of us is perfect by nature and therefore we are all 'unnatural' to some extent. Through Christ of course we are learning to be more 'natural' in terms of God's standard and one day in glory we shall be 'like Him'. It is important to understand this because some have said that Paul is only condemning the pagan permissive society in Rome where people would give up their heterosexual relationships and get involved in homosexuality simply for the sake of trying something different. Such a viewpoint is assuming that the word 'natural' means natural to the individual not to God. This is not the context of Romans 1; Paul is looking at creation and what has happened to it. Others have argued that Paul is simply condemning promiscuous homosexual behaviour, not loving and committed relationships. This is a complete misunderstanding, once again, of the context of Romans 1. Paul is making no distinction between motives behind such behaviour; he knows only too well how easy it is for us to go the way of our sinful nature and its desires, rather than obey God. For example, later in the same letter he says, 'We know that the law is spiritual; but I am unspiritual, sold as a slave to sin. I do not understand what I do. For what I want to do I do not do, but what I hate I do . . . ' (Rom. 7.14, 15). The Apostle knows only too well how difficult it is to cope with our 'unnatural' desires.

In 1 Corinthians 6. 9–11, Paul uses a couple of Greek words that have caused a lot of confusion and heartache for Christians. Many of the Bible translations do not make the meaning at all clear. Paul tells the Corinthian Christians, 'Do you not know that the wicked will not inherit the kingdom of God? Do not be deceived: Neither the sexually immoral nor idolaters nor adulterers nor male prostitutes nor homosexual offenders nor thieves nor the greedy nor drunkards nor slanderers nor swindlers will inherit the kingdom of God'.

Two Greek words 'malakos' and 'arsenokoites' are translated 'male prostitutes' and 'homosexual offenders' in the NIV. Here malakos seems to refer to either a passive partner in a homosexual act or a catamite (homosexual prostitute). Arsenokoites is very rare and may have even been invented by Paul himself (Paul also uses it in 1 Timothy 1.10, which is a list of sins linked with the ten commandments). The first part 'arsen' means male, the second half 'koite' can mean 'going to bed with' or 'chambering'. Paul appears to be describing fairly graphically a homosexual *act* between two men. Sadly so many of the translations simply say 'homosexuals' or 'homosexual perverts', which could imply anyone with a homosexual orientation or feelings. This is not what Paul is saying, any more than if 'adulterer' or 'fornicator' described anyone with heterosexual feelings. So it is the homosexual *act* which is not compatible with membership of God's Kingdom. Paul goes on to say, 'And that is what some of you were. But you were washed, you were sanctified, you were justified in the name of the Lord Jesus Christ and by the Spirit of our God' (1 Cor. 6.11). So there were people in the Corinthian Church who had been involved in a homosexual lifestyle, but were no longer.

There are many counter-arguments over this passage, as you might imagine. I have heard one person say that it is only *promiscuous* homosexuality that is being condemned, because the words imply those with more than one partner. This is ridiculous – there is no such distinction here. Given the above definitions of Paul's Greek he could just as easily be condemning a long-lasting homosexual relationship, even if it is loving and stable.

The only arguments that are really consistent are those which deny the authority of Scripture. They would agree that Paul condemns homosexual behaviour, but claim he did not understand homosexuality and was prejudiced. In other words, what Paul says is not the word of God. The debate with this viewpoint therefore rests on what authority we give to

Scripture. I have found that once you come to this position, you also have to say that heterosexual behaviour outside marriage is permissible. So then, how is adultery and fornication defined? What is the meaning of marriage? and so on. Once you start breaking through God's moral framework, it seems to me there are real problems if you want to be honest and consistent.

However, I believe it is reasonable for people to question why homosexual relationships should be wrong if a deep love and commitment are involved. Is it not simply a further expression of that love? After all, Scripture says 'God is love. Whoever lives in love lives in God, and God in him' (1 John 4.16b). This must be one of the most misinterpreted verses in Scripture. It is not saying that if something is a loving, emotional feeling . . . or even unselfish and sacrificial, it is necessarily of God. God's standards of love are defined: 'This is how God showed his love among us: He sent his one and only Son into the world that we might live through him . . . ' (1 John 4.9). If an act is not in accordance with God's will or his commands, it is not loving in terms of the Lord's definition of love. So, wherever homosexuality is mentioned in Scripture it is always in terms of a sexual act; always in the context of other (usually 'more acceptable') sins and always condemned.

Why should God say that homosexual relationships are wrong? In some ways this is difficult to understand, if we are honest. I know that for some time I did not really ask this question – I just accepted that it was wrong. It was not until I had been a Christian for some years that my thinking in this area started to develop. I began to understand something of what is meant by a 'one flesh' relationship.

In Genesis 1.27, Scripture says that 'God created man in his own image, in the image of God he created him; male and female he created them.' Then in the parallel account beginning at Genesis 2.18 we read 'The Lord God said, "It is not good for the man to be alone. I will make a helper suitable for him." . . . . So the Lord God caused the man to fall into a deep sleep; and while he was sleeping, he took one of the man's ribs [or part of the man's side] and closed up the place with flesh. Then the Lord God made a woman from the rib he had taken out of the man, and he brought her to the man'.

Something different had happened in the creation process. The woman was originally part of the man and was now brought back to him in a special 're-union', which is marriage (v. 24) 'For this reason a man will leave his father and mother and be united to his wife, and they will become one flesh.' The bodies were obviously designed for that special 're-union' and sexual intercourse was to be a celebration of it, as well as for the procreation of children. But there were other aspects of that one flesh relationship: it involved life-long commitment and it had to be between a male and a female, as in the beginning. Hence any heterosexual relationship outside marriage cannot be one flesh theologically, although it may be physically. Also, a homosexual relationship, even one that involves a life-long commitment, cannot be 'one flesh' physically *or* theologically – because it involves two of the same sex. Any sexual relationship outside this special 'one flesh' marriage is condemned by God, because it profanes his image in mankind (Gen. 1.27) and goes against his creation ideal and although since that time mankind has 'fallen', God remains firm in standing by his standard for the sexual relationship only within marriage.

Having said that, God loves us so much that he does not want sexual problems and frustrations to be a part of our experience. Underlying our sexual problem are unmet needs, nearly always rooted in our emotions. We have to find where these unmet needs lie and how God wants to meet them. I will be looking at this area in the next chapter, as I share more of what God has been teaching me personally and through others I have met in this ministry.

However, there is an important starting point in the journey towards wholeness and fulfilment in Christ. That is defining our self-identity. As I said earlier, Scripture does not conceive of sexuality as a means of identity and neither should we. Our identity must be found in the Lord Jesus Christ. That sounds obvious, but it is not quite as simple. I am referring to more than a concept, but an experience. It is a part of our Christian spirituality to learn to see ourselves as God sees us, through the cross of Christ. When we have come to God in repentance, through Jesus, we are counted as righteous in him. 'This righteousness from God comes through faith in Jesus Christ to all who believe' (Rom. 3.22). This means we are sons and daughters of God. He does not see us as homosexuals or heterosexuals in the worldly sense. God's standard of heterosexuality is very different from our human experience of it. Before the Fall, there was a sexual purity of which we know very little today (Gen. 2.25). So we need to find our identity as children of God, rather than as heterosexuals or homosexuals. That is not to say that we should deny our sexual feelings and temptations, but they need not be our identity, thanks to Jesus. We can learn to take on our new identity, which we will one day experience fully with the Lord. What is that as far as sexuality is concerned? In Mark 12.18–27, the disciples ask about marriage in heaven. Jesus says, 'When the dead rise, they will neither marry nor be given in marriage . . . ' (v. 25). Whatever our sexuality is to be in heaven, it is not hetero-sexuality as we know it on earth. So we live on earth in our human bodies, seeking to serve and follow the Lord, as Jesus did, in touch with our human feelings, or nature.

However, it is our inheritance in Christ, which is our true identity. The identity we will one day experience fully when we go to be with our Lord.

The implications of this are very far-reaching in terms of personal healing and wholeness, and must affect our self-acceptance. However, there is another vital area, linked with this. If I define my identity as a 'non-practising' homosexual or heterosexual, then I am going to feel that I am suppressing what is my real self. This causes a subtle, but strong pressure on me to conform to what I feel is my 'real self' whilst not wanting to. For many Christians who have never been involved in a homosexual lifestyle there is a curiosity or even a strong desire to see what it is like. Somehow they feel that they are missing out on something in life, which is not surprising if, subconsciously, their sexuality is their means of identity. This is quite a big problem for many Christians who contact us. The experience of this 'new identity' in Christ which I believe Scripture shows us, does not come overnight. It needs working at as part of our Christian growth.

This growth towards being what God wants us to be is the road towards healing for the person with homosexual feelings, as well as the person with heterosexual feelings. We must affirm that transformation and change are possible with God, but it is an ongoing process for us all, in different ways, because we are different people. Many will experience a change from homosexual to heterosexual leanings, others will not. Whatever our sexuality, temptation will not be a problem when we know the wholeness and fulfilment that Jesus longs for us to experience.

9: Growing in the Ministry

Having settled in a new home with my father, the ministry based in my little office (the outhouse!) was still growing, slowly but positively. Following the brief crisis of faith I now felt more secure, but thought that it would be good to do some more in-depth theological study. I felt this would strengthen my self-confidence, especially when faced by theological students. But how would it be possible? It was suggested to me that I should go away to college for a while. Several friends thought this was a good idea, although I could see many wondering if it would be a step into the ordained ministry. This appealed to a lot of people, I think possibly because it seemed respectable and secure. I would get comments like, 'Martin, I can really see you in a dog collar.'

Eventually it was decided that I should do a Diploma in Theology for two years at Oak Hill College, London. This seemed an obvious choice, mainly because David Field was there, and I felt that I could probably keep the ministry 'ticking over' and study at the same time. I applied for a grant, but was turned down. 'What was the Lord saying?' I wondered. Then my father offered to pay the tuition fees, from his life savings. Yet another example of his amazing generosity. I now felt certain that this was what I wanted to do. If I am honest, I was beginning to feel in something of a rut and rather bored, stale and lonely. The idea of this new experience, away from home and surrounded by lots of students, really appealed. By this time I had tasted quite a lot of student life through my visits to colleges and friends I made there. Needless to say, my motives for going to Oak Hill were certainly mixed, although I was determined not to see that at the time.

The college is set in lovely wooded grounds, the trees having been planted when the main house was used as a family residence. Having also at one time been partly a small farm, the estate is like a rural oasis in the centre of prosperous North London suburbia. Several buildings have been added to the main house, including a 'New Wing' which is where all the single student accommodation is. Many of the married students are housed in the modern housing estate built in the grounds, some of which have been converted from the farm buildings. It was exciting to be shown to my own room. It was obviously purpose built, with highly polished block floors, fitted light oak cupboards and a bookshelf, above which was a very large noticeboard. Although the rooms in the new wing were built in the sixties, the desks and chairs were a wide variety of shapes and sizes. It is always fascinating to see how personal souvenirs, posters and plants transform these rooms to the individual's personality. I put my magnificent large, light oak desk in the window which overlooked the croquet lawn with squirrels playing in the nearby trees and the field beyond, inhabited by a few cows.

When David Wheaton, the Principal, gave me a verse of Scripture in my welcoming interview I realised its significance to me. It was 2 Timothy 1.13, 'Guard the good deposit that was entrusted to you – guard it with the help of the Holy Spirit who lives in us.' It seemed clear that God was saying that TFT must not be neglected. I had the TFT mail forwarded to me at college and it was not long before my vision for the ministry was revitalised, largely, I am sure, due to the love and interest from other students.

I learnt so much during my time at college, especially about relationships. Before long, I noticed a slight sense of fear towards me, from many of the students, despite their love, concern and friendliness. We had a rota for meeting together in twos for prayer and some of the men shared this fear with me, often saying they felt a bit threatened by me. For example, some had been involved in homosexuality at school and had an underlying fear that they might have homosexual leanings. Others were troubled because a homosexual had made a pass at them. Sometimes their response had been one of real anger and they felt guilty about it. With others it seemed that the person making advances to them had thought they were also homosexual, and this left them feeling a little bit insecure about their own sexuality. I was able to explain that many homosexuals indulge in the wishful thinking that someone they like is also homosexual. These conversations with students opened my eyes to very understandable fears in others that I was hitherto unaware of. It helped me to understand one of the possible reasons for the lack of deep relationships in my own church fellowship.

One of my fellow students, Nigel, was aware of this problem and made a determined effort to get to know me as a person, rather than 'the man with the ministry to homosexuals'. I always found it difficult to make a move towards someone else in terms of friendship because when I make a move there is often no response. Nigel recognised this and made it a goal to get to know me. I am so grateful that he did, as we became very close friends and I value his deeply loving wisdom and openness very much indeed. It was lovely to have someone to 'drop in on', or go out with once again. Nigel was a few years younger than me; he was a tall, dark and solidly built man and his quiet, gentle manner and deep desire to understand people made him a person to whom many students turned to share anxieties and frustrations.

Because the ministry continued to grow and develop, it soon became clear that it would not be right to use my father's money for another year at college. I needed to absorb as much of the academic influences as possible, but could not complete the full course adequately and maintain the ministry of TFT. One or the other would have to go. Since I left Oak Hill many of the relationships I made there have been kept up and for me a lot of that 'family feeling' still remains, especially when I return, as I do regularly.

During my time at Oak Hill there were some significant developments in the ministry. I was now in contact with similar ministries in the USA. It was encouraging to see how the Lord had led so many of us, independently, down very similar paths of ministry. I was especially glad to have contact with 'Love in Action', a ministry based in San Rafael (near San Francisco). Some people from 'LIA' moved into the London area during my time at Oak Hill, in the hope of starting a ministry there. This never materialised at that time, but the links established were to prove very significant later.

I also met Elizabeth Moberly, a Christian psychologist, during my time at Oak Hill. Elizabeth was writing a book, following several years of research. She had come to some very positive conclusions about the causes of homosexual development and was attracted to our ministry because of our emphasis on meeting emotional needs. She came to visit me at Oak Hill and we shared our ideas. I was immediately struck by this young woman's personality and tremendous intelligence. A few years earlier I think this would have been very difficult for me to handle, but with some college experience under my belt I no longer felt threatened by academics.

Trying to put it very simply, Elizabeth believes that 'the homosexual condition involves legitimate developmental needs, the fulfilment of which has been blocked by an underlying ambivalence to members of the same sex.' She says that it is these legitimate same-sex developmental needs, which have, to various degrees, not been met by the parent of the same sex and have developed into a homosexual desire. She emphasises that the parent should not be held to blame, because the relationship problems could be in the parent, the child or a complex combination of both. It could even have resulted from an early hurt in the child's experience, not always easy to identify. This usually causes a defensive detachment from the parent of the same sex and a closer attachment to the parent of the opposite sex. This made quite a lot of sense to me, but I was not totally convinced. I can see now that there are a lot of factors involved in this highly complex sexual developmental process – different in each person's experience. I do recommend Elizabeth's book, *Homosexuality: A New Christian Ethic* (James Clarke, Cambridge) for further study.

Elizabeth believes the way forward is that the person with homosexual feelings needs to experience affirming, same-sex relationships in adulthood. This should make good the developmental deficit and encourage growth towards heterosexuality. One of the major problems is defining the precise quality of these relationships. Deep 'homo-emotional' feelings will almost certainly be there. Much of the healing will involve working through these feelings to a point of emotional security. A lot of hurts, fears and insecurities from the past will need ministry. 'Inner healing' in many forms, along with other forms of Christian counselling and ministry will be involved. TFT has always sought to understand and where necessary use, whatever form of help the Holy Spirit makes available. It is a challenge to all of us because wholeness and healing always need working through in the everyday situation.

As I learned more about myself and others, I could see the truth in Elizabeth's ideas and it underlined even more the need for understanding and experience in terms of relationships in the Body of Christ. The need to be affirmed, wanted, needed (i.e. one's love to be accepted) are very important for us all. I certainly recognise these needs in me. Right at the start of the ministry I had a letter from one of the Sisters of Mary, which was a word from the Lord for me. She said I needed a mature brother in Christ with whom to share fellowship, to the point of not making any major decision without this brother's knowledge. I knew my heart longed for such a brother. My personal life and ministry seemed dogged by loneliness. Was it the path the Lord had planned for me? Was I to learn through it total dependence on his love to meet all my needs? I am sure I still needed to experience more of that surrender to Christ, but also knew that God's love and security was to be experienced through his people.

I had wondered for a while about the possibility of bringing together people who contacted us for sharing Bible study and fellowship, the main purpose in this being to strengthen and encourage each other, with the hope of experiencing more open relationships within our own fellowships. I obviously had some fears about the possible sexual temptations this kind of group could encourage, but felt they needed to be worked through. It also seemed very important to me that not all members of the group should be from a homosexual background.

The root of problems experienced by Christians contacting me were also shared by many people with heterosexual feelings. I found a lot of Christians without experience of homosexuality could identify with my feelings and emotions. There is a tendency to believe that only someone with a homosexual orientation can identify with another homosexual. This is not true; two homosexuals may have a same-sex attraction in common, but very little else. Their fears, insecurities, hurts, sexual frustrations and habits may be quite different. On the other hand a person with heterosexual feelings may well be able to identify in all these areas. Christians (whatever their sexuality) rarely find this out, because they do not seek to relate to someone else on this level. It is often just assumed that the other cannot identify with 'my feelings', because our sexual orientation is not the same.

We called these groups 'Harbinger Groups' and had our first meeting in London. About seven or eight people turned up on the Saturday evening, it was a bit tense at first as this kind of meeting was a totally new experience for most of us. The sharing was not on a very deep level and this was to be an ongoing problem in the fortnightly Harbinger Groups. However, the time of talking over items for prayer at the end of the meeting seemed the most productive aspect. It provided a time of mutual sharing which happened naturally and usually made the meetings finish late. We decided to cut down the Bible study, which had been intended as a springboard for sharing, to give more time for prayer needs. These meetings continued in London for four years, although latterly they were infrequent, because it was difficult for me to be there. Now they have been replaced by a new London ministry called Turnabout.

During my time at Oak Hill in 1980 the Church of England's Board of Social Responsibility published a very controversial report, called 'Homosexual Relationships', which was debated in General Synod (the government of the Church of England). The report was produced by people from a mainly 'liberal' persuasion in terms of biblical authority. It was hardly surprising that they did not come out with a clear 'no' to homosexual relationships. The row within the Church of England was tremendous and Synod would not come to a decision and say where the Church stood on this issue. It was a busy time for TFT, as many churches and church groups were encouraged to look at the subject. We sent a duplicated letter and article to all the members of the Synod and the students at Oak Hill were a tremendous help in addressing letters. A few of us went to Church House and put them in the members' pigeon holes. We then stayed for the debate. It was very encouraging to hear the late Hugh Silvester (who was on our Council of Reference), mention TFT and myself in a very sensitive and moving speech.

I missed Oak Hill very much although it was good to feel more invigorated to continue the ministry of TFT. My first step was to make my long bedroom at home into a bedroom/study, with a couple of easy chairs, neatly positioned at forty-five degrees (the recognised position for counselling!). I tried to disguise my bed by rolling up the continental quilt and covering it with a tartan rug, to make it look like a settee! It was not very convincing, but it did seem a bit odd to take a rather nervous client into the bedroom to talk about his or her sexual problems! I think my improvisation helped a bit and it was great to work in a more comfortable setting than the out-house I used initially.

Our contacts and support continued to increase, but they were still mainly men, rather than women.

While I was at Oak Hill, Mike, a minister from near Manchester, began to show a lot of interest and support for our ministry. When I arrived home I met Mike, who shared a lot about a close friend of his, Peter. He was married with two children and another on the way. Mike was very concerned indeed about Peter's homosexual problems. His wife Annette knew about them, but even so their marriage was in a pretty bad way at that time. I met Mike several times but he seemed unable to persuade Peter to meet me. Then, one day in July 1980 he succeeded. Peter was a fair-haired twenty-five year old and obviously nervous. He was a bit reluctant to share at first and so, as usual, I told him a little about myself. He found it especially easy to identify with my experiences of relationships and this helped him to talk about his problems with another Christian man, and this meant a lot to him. I can remember trying to steer him away from negative feelings. It seemed a very delicate situation and I was nervous of any words or attitude on my part which could possibly cause him to reject totally what I was saying and go right away from his marriage and the Lord: thankfully, neither happened. It seems strange, looking back, how our lives have both moved on since that initial meeting. Little did I appreciate the significance of it as Peter was to become my best friend and came to work with me. Many times I would meet people in the course of TFT work and wonder if this might be the person the Lord wants as the 'brother in Christ' described by Sister Eulalia and prayed for by so many of our supporters. As usual, with God's blessings in my experience, they come when least expected.

Peter maintained contact with the ministry, as did Mike and we all became close friends. We decided to form a Harbinger Group in the North West and started fortnightly meetings in my house. As in London, it was difficult to encourage the ten or twelve attending to share very openly. I often felt I had to 'set the pace', which was a bit daunting and challenging.

I was determined to help myself feel less isolated in the ministry and therefore introduced a membership scheme, so that supporters could feel more committed and involved. The idea behind this was for members to contribute ideas, articles and testimonies for our mailing and possibly also have some contact with one another, although that was emphasised less. The other fairly radical change was the introduction of a working party for the ministry. This was made up of Christians who would meet with me regularly, bringing ideas and plans for the future direction of TFT. Anything very radical was to be approved by the trustees, before being acted upon. The working party would also be able to bring their various gifts to particular areas of the ministry. In future I would be a member of the working party and so, it was hoped, not feel as isolated. The trustees happily agreed to this idea, especially as Roy Barker had moved to Cambridge to be Director of Pastoral Studies at Ridley Hall Theological College. This meant that he was not as readily available, for instant advice and guidance.

The working party was formed with nine members, although as we progressed, some dropped out and new members were added. The major problem, as far as I was concerned, was that they were all at least forty miles away. However Peter and Mike were both members and also involved in our North West Harbinger Group, so we did see one another more frequently. They were gradually becoming the 'mainstays' of the team and probably closer to me than anyone else. Peter had been very reluctant to accept my invitation to join at first, though I was convinced that it would be good for him and for us. The sense of purpose and achievement in being used by the Lord would help boost his confidence in himself and God. I had certainly experienced that myself, even though at times I had felt very weak and unworthy. I could identify with the sense of weakness and unworthiness that Peter was experiencing, but could break through this barrier – 'You, O Lord, keep my lamp burning; my God turns my darkness into light. With your help I can run through a barricade; with my God I can scale a wall' (Ps. 18.28, 29).[1]

The Lord had shown me several times, when I was feeling at my weakest and believing I was unable to minister to others, that he wanted to use me at that very time, rather than when I felt strong again. I am not saying this is always God's way, of course. He does not want us to feel continually crippled, but at times our weakness becomes our strength in ministering Christ's love and understanding to others (2 Cor. 12.9, 10). There have been times in my ministry when, if I had the choice, I would have avoided counselling situations, because of feeling unworthy. However, the Lord did not give me the chance of 'opting out' and made me aware of how much he wanted my ministry in a specific situation. This was very humbling and made me so aware of God's love that I was greatly blessed and then more determined to obey and follow him. Having said that, I now appreciate the problems which can arise when, rather than being encouraged because we have been used in our weakness, we become even more depressed. This is because Satan, the accuser and deceiver, brings us under condemnation, often calling us hypocrites, when we are not. How we need the encouragement and affirmation of God's people! Peter eventually became one of the most valuable members of the working party, although he was probably unaware of it at the time. Through frequent telephone

[1]Incorporates NIV footnote.

conversations we were able to encourage one another. I know this was true on my part, as he gently nursed me through a few difficult patches. It was good to have a confessor in him.

With the help of the working party we were able to organise our first conference, called 'Learning to Love', which we held in the Church Hall at Upton. This was a great success and especially in the quality of worship, which we have always seen as a priority for a helpful conference. In this first, 'Learning to Love' conference, my friend from college, Nigel, spoke on 'Sexuality and the Single Person' and met his future wife Linda! How wonderful it has been to see them grow together. Also a UCCF Travelling Secretary from Manchester, Chris Medcalf, who had previously invited me to speak to a CU, came to this conference and just as we were clearing up at the end, turned to me and said timidly, 'I guess you realise my interest in this subject is more than academic!' Chris now heads up the ministry in London, Turnabout.

The ministries in the USA, similar to TFT eventually organised themselves into a coalition, called Exodus. There were now also a couple of ministries in Europe, primarily in Holland, who were similar to us. In fact they had been in existence before we arrived on the scene, although I had not known about them. Our friends in Holland organised a conference, which they called Exodus International – Europe and a few of us from the working party, including Peter and his wife Annette, went along and Geoffrey Percival, from Pilot, also joined us. This was to be quite a breakthrough in terms of Annette's involvement in the ministry. The Lord exposed many of her understandable insecurities and brought a healing and a sense of feeling able to be a part of this ministry.

I had been talking and sharing a lot about relationships and the way in which God can meet many of our needs through them, but I was conscious of not really living the kind of lifestyle I was encouraging as part of the healing process. Then a young student came to see me. He had been told to come by his tutor at Bible College, as a condition for his remaining there. He was obviously hurting and said he had been through general counselling, 'deliverance' and 'inner healing' sessions. None of them seemed to have worked and he was very disillusioned with evangelicalism. As he talked, it became very evident that he was crying out for love and I shared with him the road, in terms of Christian love and affection, I believed God wanted him to travel. Then my safe and secure position as a counsellor was shattered as he said, 'Well, you've been saying all this about what I should be experiencing, is it possible for you to show me some love and affection?' 'Help!' I thought, 'How on earth do I respond? If I say "No" to him, he will just dismiss all that I have said and accuse me of the same hypocrisy as some of the other evangelicals he knows. On the other hand . . . is what he is suggesting professional?' I was confused, but felt at least I must try to offer him something different, otherwise he was quite likely in his present frame of mind to join the 'gay church', so I nervously took the plunge and entered into a close friendship with this man. Needless to say, all this was totally unprofessional conduct on my part and the friendship was certainly not right in the way it developed, despite the fact that I insisted on total honesty about any sexual arousal either of us might feel in order to avoid our relationship travelling in the wrong direction.

After my initial hesitation the relationship deepened and I found that I was being helped and comforted by this friend's tender affection. I had not experienced anything like this for a number of years, and found that the love and affirmation I received took the lid off my emotions. We became very emotionally involved with one another. I must

129

have grieved the Lord in many ways, although my convictions and position in the ministry did prevent sexual intercourse taking place.

Eventually my friend ended our relationship, having become aware, as I think I was, that it could not continue in the direction it was going. We were both hurt, but had the friendship continued it would have meant the end of my involvement with TFT not to mention a right relationship with God. This episode did, however, serve to reveal needs in me – needs for love, affection and commitment – which were much stronger than I had imagined. Was this really what Elizabeth Moberly was talking about? How did God want to meet these deep rooted needs, some of which had been freshly exposed? The support of Peter and other members of the working party at this time was invaluable. The complex and difficult area of deeply committed Christian relationships was being opened up to us. How were our theories, if they were right, going to be put into practice? After eight years as a Christian, I thought I knew quite a lot about relationships in the Lord. It seemed I was only beginning to scratch the surface.

As the Lord increased the number of men and women prepared to help in the ministry, so people contacted us with problems which only our new helpers could really understand. For example, more women were now in touch with us and not surprisingly their experiences were often very different from the male counterparts. We met married women unaware of any homosexual feelings until their thirties or forties. A typical situation would be one in which a married woman developed a close relationship with another female. She would suddenly become aware of strong sexual and emotional feelings towards this woman and would be horrified to think she might be 'homosexual'. Women with homosexual feelings seem to be especially prone to very strong emotional dependency, although of course it also happens with men, if they allow it to happen. It is so often a question of agonising it through before God, knowing that a relationship which usurps our dependence on him is at risk. A degree of dependence in terms of security and commitment is necessary, but we have to be on our guard against idolatry and, of course, possible sexual involvement. That is why we need someone uninvolved with the situation, a committed Christian, who can help us to live in the light and bring our feelings and actions to God. This person needs to know all that is happening.

Several of our contacts were considering marriage and this was an area in which Peter and Annette were able to counsel and advise. We already knew of a few men who married thinking it would solve all their homosexual problems. The result was often a disastrous marriage relationship. On the other hand, once people from a homosexual background were finding the temptations decreasing, and sometimes even ceasing, relationships with Christian women were developing. This would start as a friendship in which both people were very honest about their feelings and problems. An emotional bond would develop and sometimes an awareness of sexual feelings for each other. In marriages which develop from this beginning, it seems that the husband with homosexual feelings is aware of a sexual desire for his wife, but not for other women. There is usually still a potential for homosexual feelings, in some cases more than others. We can always hold out the possibility of marriage for someone from a homosexual background, but it must be entered into very carefully and prayerfully. Never should marriage be considered as the answer for homosexual difficulties. In fact, heterosexual relations in marriage can actually bring homosexual feelings to the surface all the more.

We were becoming increasingly aware of the strong part the enemy, Satan, plays in sexual problems. Nearly every person we met had been taunted by the accuser and deceiver. Before every public meeting, there were problems and difficulties; in secret and vulnerable areas Satan capitalises as much as possible. We were learning to recognise this and fight against him. There is no reason why Satan should be victorious, when Christ has defeated him, through his blood shed on the cross of Calvary.

One of the best ways to stop the enemy capitalising on secrecy is to 'live in the light' with another brother or sister in Christ. This should be someone who knows and loves us. We must be aware that what we have to share will often hurt, especially if it involves sin or even temptation. This gives us an incentive to avoid difficult situations and refrain from playing with temptation because we know it will have to be shared with someone we love. I was soon to find this tremendously valuable in my relationship with Peter (James 5.16).

In 1982, my brother died suddenly, in his chair, while watching television. He had a heart attack. Most of my father's friends said it was 'a happy release for him'. Certainly his life over the last decade had been one of a recluse, rarely leaving his flat. His problems had caused a tremendous financial and emotional drain on my parents. He almost seemed to want to destroy all his friendships. I felt sad, that, at his funeral only two of his close friends who were there said they would miss him. He had taught us all a lot, despite the difficulties.

10: Vision of a Family

Early in my Christian experience I was aware of some of the problems facing single people in the Church. One way through this, I thought could be a development on the idea of Christian community, although I felt the traditional idea of Christian community discouraged individuality. I wondered if it would be possible for people to live together in a large house, each with their own bed-sitting room, but meeting together in communal rooms. In this way the individual could express his or her personality and even entertain to some extent in their own room. However they would also eat, relax and entertain with other members of the household.

As the ministry developed, the importance of the right sort of Christian relationships was apparent, both through my own experiences and those of people contacting us. I knew the sort of relationship for which I longed and believed it to be honouring to the Lord. Although I felt I could cope with more than one close relationship (a lot would be impossible to handle emotionally), there did not seem to be anyone in my own life at this time.

When Peter was a teenager and struggling with his homosexual problems, he cried to the Lord one night and God told him that some day he would be helping people with similar problems to his own. Since becoming more involved with TFT Peter had wondered several times if he should be more fully involved. At one stage I thought about the possibility of opening a coffee shop, with Peter, Annette and myself working together and also with TFT. Peter was unemployed at the time but the door to this plan was quite firmly closed. Then he managed to get a job and soon started buying his own house. However, the thought of a return to full-time Christian work was always there. He knew the job he had with a petrol station company would not last forever and it seemed that when eventually it did come to an end, then would be the time to think again about Christian work.

Peter and I had encouraged and ministered to one another as we both tasted something of Christian relationships. We were both looking for a person or people who would meet the same-sex emotional needs that Elizabeth Moberly felt were so important. In the closeness that was beginning to develop between Peter, myself and increasingly, Annette, we mentioned the idea of community from time to time, but only semi-seriously. Peter had always been impressed by some Christians he knew in Eastbourne who lived together as a large family and ministered the love of Christ to many people from their home. In Christmas 1982, Peter, Annette and the children stayed at my house over the New Year. They had been keen to cancel the whole idea, wondering how in earth they would cope with the children and my father in such a close atmosphere. The Lord certainly overruled in the situation and it was quite a success. Again, only half seriously, we wondered if this was a foretaste of community living!

The time came when some positive steps had to be taken. Peter's job was soon to end and Philip, his eldest son, was due to move schools, in September, 1983. Peter and Annette did not want him to start at this school and then be uprooted. We prayed about it and I talked over the idea with my father. He was amazing, and said he would fall in with our plans and did not want to stand in the way. We all felt it would help bring a new dimension to his life and hopefully end some of the loneliness he was experiencing. Where would we live? I found a few possible houses in the Birkenhead area, but there seemed to be nothing in Rochdale, where they were living. If we were to live together it looked as if it would be in Birkenhead. We decided to 'lay a fleece' before the Lord, so that if it was right there would be a buyer for our house by June, 1983 (this was at Eastertime of that year).

Both Peter and I knew that one of our reasons for living together like this would be to help meet our emotional needs and in doing that provide an environment of love in the home and between us all, which visitors could see and experience. Hence the answers we believe God has for the person with homosexual problems would be seen in action, rather than simply in theory.

I had been asked to be President of Exodus International – Europe and was given the job of organising the May 1983 conference. We chose Ashburnham Place in Sussex and thought we would try to get Jim Bigelow, from the USA as our main speaker, with 'Loving Relationships in the Body of Christ' as our subject. Jim had written an excellent book called *Love Has Come Again*, but I doubted that he would be available for our conference. Contacting him was really a 'shot in the dark', so I was really thrilled when he accepted. We also invited Elizabeth Moberly to speak on homosexuality and trans-sexuality.

The conference was a success and I found Jim's talks especially encouraging. I was able to share with him a little of my own experiences, ideas and hopes as well as fears and he encouraged me a lot. I still had some reservations about

135

relating on a deep emotional level to a married man like Peter. In some ways, the future still seemed almost unreal because no positive moves and decisions had yet been made. However, there was a growing bond of love between us.

When June arrived we had two potential buyers for the house and both could complete the transaction. We felt the Lord was saying that we should proceed with caution. By this time, Peter had been made redundant and Annette took on a job as manager for a household container firm. This provided a car as well as some additional income. Peter was able to come over to Birkenhead for the day now and again to help out with office work. Our relationship started to develop and there was a sense of commitment for the future. He was showing me love and affection that meant a lot. I knew there was no sexual attraction there and I was not aware of strong feelings in that direction either. I especially remember one incident when they were all going away to France for a holiday provided by someone we met at Ashburnham. Before they left, Peter said, 'It doesn't seem fair, somehow, I feel you should be coming as well.' It meant so much to know of this love and commitment to me.

The sale of our house was fraught with problems. There was always a potential buyer, but then at the last minute it would fall through, and it sometimes seemed as if the Lord was opening a door for us and then shutting it. Despite all this, it did seem clear that God was saying 'go ahead', because the situation on the house sale never completely fell through. Whenever we questioned whether our plans were right with God, a 'door' would open again and encourage us to continue. Eventually it became clear that a positive decision regarding the move would have to be taken because of Philip's schooling. He would have to be transferred to Birkenhead by September 1983 and so Peter and Annette decided to move Philip over to his new school. He would stay in our house with Peter, myself and my father and Annette and the other children would stay in their house until it was sold and our new home together was found. This was to be longer than we anticipated, but there is no doubt it was a part of the Lord's plan, because it served several purposes. Although it was a difficult time of separation for Peter and Annette, it strengthened their marriage relationship. It also brought a new closeness to Peter and Philip's relationship. This important time helped my father, Peter and Philip to get to know one another and of course Peter and I had to work at our relationship together in this very special situation. God had been good to us, because many of the additional pressures of home and family life were taken away. There were of course problems: Peter and his family obviously missed one another during the week. This situation was to continue until May, 1984.

Now I really was beginning to find how little I really did know about loving in the Lord Jesus. I am sure the mistakes that I made would fill another book!

The foundations for the future were clearly being laid by the Lord and he showed us that the first step must be one of commitment, to God and to one another. Jim Bigelow had showed us that when God said, 'It is not good for the man to be alone,' (Gen. 2.18) it was while God and man still had a perfect relationship, unmarred by sin. Therefore even before the fall God was saying 'I have created you to need someone else apart from me', and we do need someone else apart from God, although of course our relationship with him is the most important. Jim also showed us how relationships we see in Scripture involved a deep commitment. For example, 'Jonathan made a covenant with the house of David . . . . And Jonathan had David reaffirm his oath out of love for him, because he loved him as he loved himself' (1 Samuel 20.16, 17). Also we have the friendship of Ruth and Naomi. 'Ruth replied, "Don't urge me to leave you or to turn back from you. Where you go I will go, and where you stay I will stay. Your people will be my people and your God my God. Where you die I will die, and there I will be buried. May the Lord deal with me, be it ever so severely, if anything but death separates you and me"' (Ruth 1.16, 17).

It may not be always right to make that sort of commitment, but something akin to it is important in a relationship of great depth. It is obviously not possible to relate to a lot of people like that. It seems from the Gospels that Jesus was especially close to just three disciples, Peter, James and John.

It gave me a great sense of personal joy and security to affirm an oath of love for Peter and Annette and to be able to substantiate that by means of a will and eventually joint house ownership. A friendship often needs a solid commitment before the Lord to hold it together, when everything around, and often the people themselves, are being torn apart. It has certainly been true in our lives.

It was not long before we discovered some of our fears and insecurities. As soon as I could see I was causing Peter to feel a bit threatened I made a conscious effort to make him feel in the same position as myself in terms of authority in the ministry. This was a mistake in many ways because Peter actually needed to feel less pressure of responsibility. I should have taken more of a positive lead, both at work and in our relationship because Peter was constantly battling with his reactions to my indecision and lack of organisation. Before long I developed a very deep love for him and with that many insecurities and fears, usually related to past incidents in my life, surfaced. I often demanded more than he could give. I was beginning to make Peter feel smothered and what started as a very open relationship, in terms of sharing problems and difficulties, started to become far less so. I often became suspicious and hurt, which in turn hurt Peter. I was also aware of stronger sexual feelings for him than were there at the beginning. Although I knew in theory that his love for me should not depend on any sexual attractiveness, I often found it difficult to believe that I was loved and sought affirmation. I knew that any sexual involvement or even interest (if it were mutual) would cause a big threat to his marriage and for that reason did not want him to find me attractive. Yet I found it difficult to believe I was loved without that. The Lord had a lot of work to do with both of us, but there were many positive areas of healing as well, during our time together. We learned a lot even though sometimes it seemed like two steps forward and two or even three steps back. I also found a great love developing for Annette.

It was wonderful to experience a partnership in the ministry. It was a great joy to know I was loved and I experienced this assurance through Peter's commitment and also in gentle signs of affection and affirmation. He learnt to know when I was hurting without my saying a word, and I could sense when *he* was under pressure or perhaps feeling threatened by a person or situation. I had never known this depth of love before.

We were, however, especially aware of the enemy's hand, bringing division and misunderstanding. This was usually related to a significant time, like a meeting or project we were undertaking. We also saw the Lord bring a tremendous reconciliation and healing, many times. If we were going to grow in the Lord we needed to understand more of him and more of one another.

Suddenly, the house situation changed dramatically. Peter

and Annette's house was sold and they had to be out by May. It at last looked as if we had a sale going through. The Lord had shown us that it would all be an 'eleventh hour' situation, which would work out in the end. We had contacted local housing associations to see if there was any chance of temporary accommodation, but they held out no hope. Then, little over a week before they were due to move out of their home, the housing association came up with an excellent four-bedroomed terraced house for a rent which was amazingly cheap and could be used as a temporary measure. Then we saw an eight-bedroomed Georgian house in Oxton which seemed ideal for us as a family. It needed a lot of work and was therefore possibly within our price range. It had been originally on the market for £79,000 but most of the fittings had since been removed. We felt it right to offer £31,000 and to our surprise they accepted. Father and I now had a sale go through on our own house with a 'first time buyer' (very unusual for this type of property). The Lord certainly had moved at the 'eleventh hour'! Peter with a lot of help from Mike, worked on the renovations and eventually, in July 1984, father and I moved into a couple of the upstairs rooms as a temporary measure.

When Peter and Annette eventually moved in there were still misunderstandings and frictions, although most of the fears that we had beforehand were not realised. The major problem was a lack of understanding as we tended to have preconceived ideas as to the way each other would react in a given situation. There was, however, a growing love and acceptance and the careless comments and misunderstandings became fewer. I was proud of my new family and learning to love Annette and the children in a very special way.

11: The Family – Hurting and Healing

A very daunting and completely different lifestyle was now beginning. Not as dramatically different as joining a community or becoming a monk, but traumatic, to say the least. I had made one of the most important decisions of my life. Was it going to work? So many Christians had written about their lives in 'extended families' and communities, often with enough negatives to put us off the idea. I am not too keen on phrases such as 'extended family' or 'community'. They sound almost clinical to me. I prefer to simply use the word 'family'. We are not closely related through our parents and grandparents, but surely the blood of Jesus and the Holy Spirit within each of us is a much closer family bond than any other? My family are my family through Jesus and our mutual commitment. Peter kept comparing our relationships with that of a newly married couple. It may sound a strange comparison to some, but how right he was.

We all moved into Fairfield Lodge with different anxieties. We sometimes convinced ourselves that problems should be there, when in fact they were not. For example, our tastes in furnishing were not all that dissimilar, when we imagined they would be poles apart. Had this not been the case, however, I was aware that my timidity could have made me accept what I did not like, for the sake of not causing any problems – a terrible reflection on my own weakness and vulnerability. In many ways I was reliving my relationships with friends in childhood. The same 'tape' was playing in my subconscious – 'I will learn to do whatever you do in order that you will accept me'. In childhood this was playing football and cricket with my friends, now it was a much more difficult game, and I felt something like a loser from the start. Nevertheless, we all kept reminding ourselves that the Lord had brought all this about for a purpose; we must trust him.

Although we emphasised that Fairfield Lodge was to be a family home, not a centre for TFT or a 'community' home we decided to have a housewarming/dedication. We organised this and eighty people attended.

The house provided us with a living room and kitchen each; a dining room and what had been a games room. This room is panelled with wood possibly from a Victorian church or chapel. Because there are no windows on the wall, but simply skylights, it is excellent for ministry and meetings. There is plenty of light from the 'peaked' roof, but also some water leaks and a lot of cold air! When we have enough money, it will be insulated and carpeted properly. At the dedication we managed to squeeze the eighty people into that room, and hear Roy Barker share God's Word for us. In his lovely way, he gave us three letters – 'OAP'. We must be 'Open' to God and one another. We would experience 'Affliction'. We must 'Persevere'. Those words have certainly proved prophetic! We sent teams of people around the house to pray in every room. We heard interesting reports on some of the prayers in the kitchens and bedrooms, especially Peter and Annette's!

There was still a lot of remedial work and alterations to

be done on the house, although the main living rooms were finished. Peter was well qualified for this type of work as an electrician and plumber (his father's trade). It was a tremendous challenge for him to take on the renovation, which meant re-fitting the sinks, baths and lavatories (all of which had been removed) and adding to them. Mike re-wired the house with him, to a very high standard. Peter had been released from TFT ministry to work on the house for six months prior to the dedication. Often working on his own, it became a heavy burden. Although one of our local supporters had very generously paid for an unemployed man to help with the redecoration, there were still tremendous pressures on Peter. I personally lacked a lot of self-confidence in the practical area, because of Peter's professionalism. In the past I had undertaken some work on houses I owned, but, in this situation, I was very conscious of my efforts not coming up to Peter's high standards. I was able to do some wall-scraping and even a little decorating, but felt very much like a nervous child seeking to please his parent. This was ironic considering Peter was twelve years younger than me. The last thing he needed at this stage, was yet another child!

Although there was still some work to be done on our home, we eventually felt it should be 'shelved', to give Peter a break and bring him back into the ministry of TFT.

TFT's ministry was still growing, during this period, but now took on a very exciting new dimension. This seemed to coincide with the publication of an article about Peter and Annette in *Family* magazine. Married couples were coming to Peter and Annette for counselling, the majority of cases being where the husband had homosexual problems. Some people contacted us as a result of the article, or simply through hearing about TFT's ministry some other way. It was a great encouragement to see the Lord developing

Peter and Annette's ministry and giving them more confidence, in very much the same way as he had for me. If he had once felt daunted by people like academics, clergy and doctors, the Lord dealt with that by bringing them to us for help! The threat disappears when you discover that they are vulnerable and hurting too. People started to come and stay at Fairfield Lodge for a few days and the Lord ministered to them there in wonderful ways. It was often when we, either individually or corporately, felt very weak and unworthy: how gracious is our God.

However, the Lord was teaching us all a lot about ourselves and, as we were ministered to by others, our own ministry developed. Needless to say, before long we all became too busy. While this was not so much of a problem for me as an individual, it laid a great deal of pressure on Peter and his family. It was difficult to escape from TFT. Annette and the children needed Peter's time, and then there was the running of the house with so many practical jobs which needed doing. If we relaxed and did nothing, we had to force ourselves not to feel guilty, especially if one of the others was busy. We decided that more structure was needed in terms of a timetable. At that stage we spent little, if any time, relaxing together and even worse we seldom prayed together, except in a crisis. We were seeking the impossible, living separately, yet together.

When my mind wasn't focused on the ministry, it was often in a state of emotional turmoil. I wanted to be a better friend to Peter and meet more of his needs. I tried, rather pathetically, to prove that I could do this and usually failed. The more I thought I had let go, the more Peter got the opposite impression. He sensed, quite naturally, how much he was on my mind and therefore the pressure of feeling smothered was there as much as ever. I was encouraged to develop other interests and relationships. I lacked a lot of enthusiasm for this. As a Christian, I felt I had tried in the past to make close friendships and it only worked a couple of times. Was this my fault? I think not entirely, but I could have persevered much more than I did.

I was on a self-defeating spiral downwards. The more I failed in my relationship with Peter and others in the house, the weaker and more insecure I felt. This caused even more pressure, especially on Peter, who felt guilty, hurt and even angry that he could not respond in the way I was demanding. I knew I was loved by Peter and Annette – it seemed ungrateful of me to want to be *needed* as well. How could they be expected to need someone who so often made them feel guilty and seemed not to appreciate the love that was already there? It often took a crisis situation to bring us to the point of sharing our feelings together and this was usually, but not always, with the help of a Christian friend, Walter. Quite often Annette and I were able to share together, but this was not always right when Peter might become the topic of our conversation. Nevertheless, there were some very positive developments in my relationship with Annette and a lot of the awkwardness (which I have often felt with women) was broken down.

I began to understand that being able to consider myself part of such a family, even as an 'adopted child', was helping me more than I realised. I no longer thought of marriage as out of the question, although it was and is not my aim, nor do I believe it is the answer to homosexuality, or a 'proof' of healing.

I was also learning to love the children very much (or perhaps I should say, the 'other children'). There were times when I was left to look after them for a few days, when I reached screaming pitch (as their parents did sometimes). However, experiencing the children's love and feeling our relationships develop was very beautiful for me.

Needless to say, my insecurities came flooding to the surface once again, when Peter met a Christian man with whom he could identify and also respect, and they became very close friends. Paul lived two and a half hours away by car and came to stay for a couple of days and then almost once a week. He was a very nice person, but I felt deeply threatened and hurt. It seemed as if I was being rejected, although of course I was not. I kept trying to convince myself that if I was really loving in the right way I should be pleased for Peter. That just seemed to increase guilt. That was how I should have felt, but I was not there yet. Sometimes, if allowed, my insecurity erupted as anger, 'It's not fair, after my struggles – living and working with someone – another person gets all the candy when I have to suffer the nitty gritty everyday difficulties.' Quite naturally, my reaction pushed Peter even further away, although he so often tried to help me. Life frequently felt like a nightmare, if only I could escape, as from boarding school, then I could cope – but facing the hurt almost every day often became unbearable.

If that was true for me then it was also true for Peter and Annette. Yet we could not escape. Learning to love is not about escaping. The Lord was allowing this for a reason, but the enemy, Satan, was also very active. He would capitalise on our vulnerabilities, especially when we were about to embark on some ministry for the Lord. Although the attacks often seemed unbearable, Christ is victorious and every time victory was experienced, usually at the last minute. For example, before a speaking engagement, I would be feeling depressed. 'How can I possibly speak to these people?' The Lord always undertook in even the seemingly impossible situations.

Where was God's healing in all this? It was there, of course. I needed to find my security in him. Sometimes I did and on one occasion experienced such a love for the Lord it was as if I had fallen in love with him all over again. At times like these everything felt so much better, but then with another crisis, it would seem we were back to the same old problems.

However, there were very positive times amid all this doom and gloom. For example, Peter and I were learning to minister together, and the Lord was beginning to heal a lot of the self-consciousness about this that had arisen out of my fears and insecurities and which had spoilt our relationship and destroyed a lot of Peter's respect for me in the past. Whilst on a visit to All Nations College we gave the students the opportunity to speak to either one of us, or both of us together. They all chose to see us together and one student actually wanted the two of us to minister to him together. Through this we were shown how we needed to release one another's ministry to the Lord. It was actually the Holy Spirit's ministry, not ours, and we had to appreciate that and not question what the other might or might not be doing. With that kind of confidence in the Lord, there was much more unity between us. Disunity had so often been caused by centering too much on our relationship and not enough on the Lord, but God was trying to show us that the fundamental problem was the same in both of us, namely a lack of self-acceptance. This is a major problem for so many Christians, although it is manifested in a multitude of ways. Guilt also plays a vital part, especially in the perfectionist, who cannot accept himself because he is not perfect.

One of the ways a lack of self-acceptance comes to the surface is when someone only feels really secure with another person who appears to be just like themselves or the way they would like to be. In my case I see in Peter something of the potential that is in me, some of the qualities I would like. On the other hand, Peter often sees quite a lot of his own weaknesses in me, weaknesses he is still trying to overcome! When this happens there is a clash. It is therefore the lack of self-acceptance in both of us which causes the problem. My lack of self-acceptance makes me want to please, which puts a lot of pressure and demands on the very people I want to please. So what is the point in all this hurting of one another, the mixture of love, hurt, anger and bitterness? It seemed, when we went to Fairfield Lodge, after the months of waiting, there was a lot of re-building work to be done in our relationships. Since then, there has been even more rebuilding necessary. Yet, through all this we have been led to seek healing for our-selves and one another. When the masks are off, we are vulnerable but God is not about demolishing, without re-building. I am constantly reminded by the Lord that I made a covenant before him in terms of a commitment to Peter and Annette. Scripture shows that such commitments are not to be taken lightly and certainly not to be broken. For example, David honoured his commitment to Jonathan, even after his death. When the Gibeonites asked for the lives of seven of Saul's descendants, David spared Jonathan's son, 'because of the oath before the Lord between David and Jonathan' (2 Sam. 21.7). Psalm 15 reminds us how important openness and honesty is in relationships as part of our commitment. The Lord honours the man, 'who keeps his oath even when it hurts'(Ps. 15.4).

I was very conscious of the ways in which Peter and Annette were seeking to help me. Our openness was developing, although I was still a bit reluctant. I was able to share difficulties (not concerning Peter) with Annette and she made it clear to me that she understood and was sensitive to my feelings. We also felt it important to involve my father more in the situation. He had obviously realised that I was depressed and sharing my feelings with him was something of a breakthrough in our relationship. God was certainly doing something with us, but it was difficult to see clearly and identify.

12: Taking a Journey

'The Lord gave me a picture of your house and it seemed to be in flames. It was under attack from outside.'

The sister who shared this with us had never seen the house before, but it became clear that her vision was an accurate one. Some of the details she described could not have been revealed to her by anyone. We accordingly shared something of our problems with this friend, and she felt we needed to have a group of people supporting us both practically and spiritually. She also pointed out the importance of worship within the house – this made sense to me as my own feelings of love and security with the Lord have frequently been rekindled in the atmosphere of worship and adoration. Our monthly 'praise meeting', which we held on a Saturday evening was developing into a regular group of about twenty. At first we used a lot of lively choruses and sought to encourage lively worship, but the atmosphere was beginning to change. As people started to feel relaxed and at home with one another, there was a little more informality and sharing. The worship tended to be gentle and subdued.

Many of the Christian counsellors we met shared their own experience within a group therapy-type support group. Counsellors need counsel and healing too! If you had not realised that before, you must now see how true it is in my situation! Perhaps these praise meetings would give birth in some way to our much needed support?

I had come a long way, in terms of learning to love God, others and myself. In fact we had all come a long way in these areas, although it seemed there was nearly always one of us in a state of hopelessness when the others were feeling more positive. And yet, whatever our feelings, the Holy Spirit led us into deeper areas of counselling for others. We were all being used by God and many people seemed so greatly helped by our ministry. However, I still fell prey to another attack of depression, this time, a really bad one. 'What's the point Lord? . . . . We aren't meeting one another's needs . . . . Please help me . . . I can't cope any more. Take me home!' My world seemed frightening and hostile but I could not run away. I realised these feelings were not right and I was being very ungrateful for all the love I had been given – but I couldn't help my reactions.

God's ways are indeed wonderful and strange. In all this gloom, there was a spark of encouragement. Tim, the person used in my conversion, had played little part in my life of late. We kept in touch, but I knew as little of what was happening in his life as he knew of mine. We began meeting together again, and he soon realised how weak, vulnerable and depressed I was. It happened that he was also going through a traumatic emotional crisis. We talked, prayed and wept together in a way that we had never done before. Weeping was becoming increasingly easier for me, which must have indicated some positive healing in that area. It seemed, after fourteen years, that Tim and I were actually getting to know one another.

A few months earlier, Peter had been to a Christian Gestalt conference. Gestalt, literally translated, means 'wholeness'. The term is more widely used to describe a number of in-depth counselling techniques used to discover the path towards wholeness. Like other areas of secular counselling, the Lord often uses it with remarkable results, when it is given to him and 'Christianised'.

Peter was greatly helped by this course and one of our supporters suggested that I should book in for the next 'Gestalt Week', which I did. At the Gestalt Conference, and at another similar conference in France which I attended immediately prior to it, I experienced the type of ministry where one is encouraged to relax and take an imaginary journey. At one stage we were asked to imagine being in a beautiful, secluded part of the countryside and later drew a picture we had seen on this trip. My sense of hopelessness was very evident in the confusion I pictured around the symbol of the cross. On another occasion we were taken on an imaginary journey down a busy main road and then off into a side street, where we saw an empty shop with just one object in it, a spinning wheel. It was a bit dusty, but very valuable. Why had it been left there? It had been abandoned by mistake. The owners had done a 'moonlight flit'. I was asked to become that object. The journey continued back to the busy main street and to a hypermarket where I could buy anything I wanted. I decided to buy something that would make me into a beautiful and acceptable person. That seemed unrealistic so I chose a convertible car, and was asked to become that object. I was a bit rusty!

These journeys, for many of us – certainly for me, were very revealing. I sought ministry from my group of eight people. Some simple prayers were offered to the Lord and I was asked to repent of sins, including a hidden one of deception. I let go and fell onto a mattress on the floor. I cannot actually remember landing on it – it seemed as if I was floating and I was filled with a tremendous sense of love for the Lord and a feeling of security. There was no embarrassment at all. The only physical sensation was a tingling throughout my body. It seemed almost like a 'spiritual blood transfusion', flowing through me. As I lay there I was encouraged by the leader to 'speak' to Peter and Annette, even though they were not present. 'Use your new blood, securely, to speak to Peter,' he coaxed. My words seemed to flow quite naturally, without any premeditation. I affirmed my love for Peter and Annette, expressing my feelings of security and acknowledging that I had a lot to give them. 'I am not your hurting child any more . . . I am a man. I am going to stand on that authority.' I also expressed my sorrow for the ways in which I had caused hurt. As I lay there, the words seemed to be coming spontaneously from my heart rather than from my mind. In some ways it was as if I was not really in control and yet I knew it was really me. The best way of describing it seemed to be as a response to the leader's direction. It was the result of my 'spiritual blood transfusion'.

The experience had a marked effect. From then on I knew I did not have to please in order to gain love and acceptance. I was fairly confident in my new-found security, but rather like a bird learning to fly, still felt a little uncertain about what had actually happened and how it would affect my life and relationships.

I travelled to Haywards Heath to attend a retreat and was joined there by Peter and Annette. How would I respond to them? How would they respond to me? There were only nine of us on the retreat, including the two leaders. It was wonderfully friendly and informal. Then we were asked if we would like to go on an imaginary journey! 'Another one!' I thought, 'Lord, what is this all about? What are you trying to do?'

This time we were asked to walk on a lonely, but moonlit path up a mountain. I took a path on the right towards a cave, where an old man greeted me. I sensed a tremendous cleanliness and purity about him, both physically and spiritually. He had immeasurable wisdom. I was told to share with him an important question on my mind, concerning the future implications of what I had experienced over the past couple of weeks. The old man gave me assurance and confidence for the future. It was going to be all right. Then I was told he would give me something. He reached into his cloth bag and put a beautiful glass egg in my hand. It was very smooth and as clear as crystal, yet it glistened with a multitude of colours reflected within. Every time I looked at it, there was something different and more beautiful to be seen. I sensed that the man had given it as a token of all that he shared with me. Yet it was more than that, it almost seemed like a kind of sacrament. I was told to become this object. This I did and it seemed to seal within me the hope the wise old man had shared. I became myself again and left to go back down the mountain with my precious egg. Just before I left the mountain path I was asked to look again at my gift and see something unnoticed before.

I looked into the beautiful glass object and saw . . . . myself! I was stunned. In fact I cannot remember any more of the journey, the revelation had such an impact on me.

'I love you, O Lord my strength. The Lord is my rock, my fortress and my deliverer: my God is my rock, in whom I take refuge. He is my shield and the horn [strength] of my salvation, my stronghold.'

(Ps. 18.1, 2)

On reflection it seemed clear that God had used these journeys to affirm within me all that had been happening over these two weeks. I was a valuable person of immense worth to God. My relationships with others could be secure on that foundation. I had known that in theory of course, but the Lord in his wonderful way, had transformed it into a vivid experience. A memory for me to preserve. Who was that infallible man on the mountain? Was it God himself? These journeys were not just a picture of what happened over two weeks, but of a lifetime.

I have learnt; I am learning; I will learn to love God, other people and myself. This healing process will only be complete when I am with Jesus. 'Now we see but a poor reflection; then we shall see face to face. Now I know in part; then I shall know fully, even as I am fully known. And now these three remain: faith, hope and love. But the greatest of these is love' (1 Cor. 13.12, 13).

APPENDIX 1: Christ's Way out of Homosexuality

1. Belief in God as revealed in Christ.
2. The recognition that God says 'No' to homosexual sex and why he does so (Genesis 2.21–24; Leviticus 18.22; Romans 1.24–28; 1 Corinthians 6.9–11).

It is always homosexual sex which is mentioned in Scripture and condemned. It is always in the context of other sins, such as greed, drunkenness and pride (anything or anyone taking God's place in our hearts). Homosexuality can never be a God ordained 'one flesh' relationship.

3. Repentance (turning away) from a homosexual lifestyle and behaviour (Acts 17.30, 31; 2 Corinthians 5.17).

Especially if there has been some involvement in a homosexual lifestyle, old behaviour patterns and anything associated with the homosexual culture must go.

4. An understanding of God's love and forgiveness (Hebrews 8.12).

A right appreciation of God as our loving heavenly Father. An experience of God's forgiveness, through the suffering of Jesus Christ on the cross. There is often a deep work of healing required to make this a fundamental part of our spirituality. Books, such as *The Father Heart of God* by Floyd McClung (Kingsway) should be helpful.

5. Finding a new identity in Christ, rather than homosexuality or heterosexuality (Romans 3.21–26; Mark 12.25).

Scripture does not identify people by their sexual feelings. We have to learn to see ourselves as God sees us, through the atoning work of Christ on the cross. This is not as a 'homosexual' or 'heterosexual' in the worldly sense. We must admit and face up to our sexual feelings but not make these our form of self-identity.

6. What are the needs that homosexuality is seeking to meet?

For example, emotional needs for love and affirmation, loneliness, lack of direction and purpose in life, lack of achievement, lack of excitement.

7. How does God want to meet these needs and heal? (Romans 12.13; John 15.12; 1 John 4.7–12).

Through our relationship with God and within the fellowship of the Body of Christ. Learning to love as Jesus loved.

8. What are the hurts, fears and insecurities which help to obstruct this healing? (Psalm 139.13–16).

When and how have we been hurt? How do we respond to ourselves and others as a result? Allowing the Holy Spirit to minister. Removing the masks.

9. The need of accountability and confession (mutual if possible); fellowship and support – giving and receiving ministry (James 5.16).

Commitment, openness, sharing with a limited number of especially close friends. Learning to love and be loved – a safeguard against temptation because the situation is going to be shared with someone else whom we love, someone who will be hurt if we fail, as God is hurt. The fulfilment of unmet needs, especially emotional ones which are the driving force behind the sexual temptation.

APPENDIX 2: Christian Agencies

(Help available for those seeking a Christian alternative to the homosexual lifestyle)

ENGLAND

True Freedom Trust, PO Box 3, Upton, Wirral, Merseyside L49 6NY (051-653-0773). A teaching and counselling ministry for all concerned with a biblical approach to homosexuality and related problems.

Turnabout, PO Box 592, London SE4 1EF (01-460-2425). Similar to TFT, but a ministry to London and the home counties.

Pilot, c/o Shankhill Road Mission, 116 Shankhill Road, Belfast BT13 2BD (0232-230743). Telephone and personal counselling. Advertisements placed in secular press.

EUROPE

Various ministries may be contacted through:
Exodus International – Europe, PO Box 3, Upton, Wirral, Merseyside L49 6NY

UNITED STATES AND CANADA

Various ministries contactable through:
Exodus International, PO Box 2121, San Rafael, CA 94912 (415) 454-1017.

AUSTRALIA

Liberty, GPO Box 2086, Brisbane, Queensland 4001, Australia.

Other Marshall Pickering Paperbacks

FORGIVE AND RESTORE

Don Baker

When a member of God's family, in this case a loved pastor, goes seriously off the rails in his personal life, the questions looms large, What should the church do about it? Is it a matter for the church leadership only? Should the wayward member be asked to leave or just relieved of responsibility? What should the congregation be told?

This book is a remarkable account of how one church dealt with such a highly charged and emotional crisis. It records in honest detail the ebb and flow of hope and despair, uncertainty and humanity, and relying throughout on biblical principles, it picks its way through a tangled mess to find a place of healing and restoration again.

WHEN YOU PRAY

Reginald East

Spiritual renewal has awakened in many Christians a deeper longing to know God more intimately. Prayer is the place where we personally meet God, yet it is often treated simply as the means for making requests for our needs, and offering our stilted, dutiful thanks. In this practical guide to prayer, Reginald East shows how we can establish a prayer relationship with God which is both spiritually and emotionally satisfying. Through understanding God and ourselves better, prayer can truly become an encounter with God, where we relax into Him, enjoy Him, listen as well as talk to Him and adventure into discovering His heart of love.

If you wish to receive *regular information* about *new books*, please send your name and address to:

London Bible Warehouse
PO Box 123
Basingstoke
Hants RG23 7NL

Name..

Address ....

....

....

....

I am especially interested in:
- ☐ Biographies
- ☐ Fiction
- ☐ Christian living
- ☐ Issue related books
- ☐ Academic books
- ☐ Bible study aids
- ☐ Children's books
- ☐ Music
- ☐ Other subjects

P.S. If you have ideas for new Christian Books or other products, please write to us too!